Statistical Treatment of Experimental Data

AN INTRODUCTION TO STATISTICAL METHODS

Treating experimental errors

Analyzing experimental data

Concept of probability

Distribution of errors

Propagation of errors

Correlations

Hugh D. Young is Assistant Professor of Physics and Head of the Department of Natural Sciences, Margaret Morrison Carnegie College, Carnegie Institute of Technology.

STATISTICAL TREATMENT
OF EXPERIMENTAL DATA

HUGH D. YOUNG

Assistant Professor of Physics
Head, Department of Natural Sciences
Margaret Morrison Carnegie College
CARNEGIE INSTITUTE OF TECHNOLOGY

McGRAW-HILL BOOK COMPANY, INC.

New York   San Francisco   Toronto   London

STATISTICAL TREATMENT
OF EXPERIMENTAL DATA

6 7 8 9 0 MPC 75 74 73 72 71 70 69 68 67

DEDICATION | To Alice,
who shares her
Wonderland
with me.

PREFACE

Every scientist and engineer needs some elementary knowledge of statistical methods for treating experimental errors and analyzing experimental observations. The basic concepts of probability, distribution of errors, propagation of errors, and correlations are an indispensable part of the knowledge of anyone who has contact with numbers related to experimental observations.

Many undergraduate engineering and science students, however, find little or no time in their curricula for an introduction to even the most elementary statistical methods. It is the author's firm belief that some of these techniques should be introduced early in the undergraduate curriculum in science or engineering, so that they may be used in later courses which incorporate laboratory work.

Accordingly, this book has been written with considerable missionary zeal in an attempt to present some of these techniques in a form which is understandable, palatable, and even enjoyable for sophomore science or engineering students with little mathematical sophistication and no previous exposure to the subject of this book. The only mathematical background assumed is a year of elementary calculus. A year of general college physics is helpful in understanding some of the illustrative examples, but is not essential.

Many of the mathematical developments are given a somewhat intuitive rather than a completely rigorous presentation. It is to be expected that this practice will be condemned by specialists in mathematical statistics, but it is followed here deliberately and without apology. The author feels strongly that the student should encounter this material at an early stage in his education rather than waiting until a more rigorous treatment is feasible. The practice of presenting useful formulas with *no* derivation at all has, however, been studiously avoided.

The author's experience in teaching this material to several generations of sophomores majoring in physics at Carnegie Institute of Technology has shown that mastery of it is not beyond the ability of students at this level. It has been incorporated into the first part of a course given students majoring in physics in the first semester of their sophomore year. Most of the material can be covered quite thoroughly in four to six weeks, with three class hours per week and homework assignments for each hour. This material is then followed by laboratory work in which the statistical methods are put to work.

Such a subcourse can be fitted into any course in the sophomore, junior, or senior year in which quantitative laboratory work plays an important part. The book is also sufficiently self-contained so that it may be used for individual study. In either case, exercise in applying the principles is essential. In addition to many illustrative examples in the text, a collection of problems has been included at the end of each chapter. A summary of important formulas is included in Appendix A.

The book is intended primarily to be read from beginning to end. Several chapters may be omitted, however, without too much loss of continuity. The reader who is interested mostly in the Gauss distribution and its consequences may omit Secs. 7, 8, and 11. Sections 10 and 16 also may be omitted if desired.

In conclusion, a statement is necessary about what the book is *not*. It is *not* a treatise of mathematical statistics. Neither is it a comprehensive discussion of all aspects of treatment of experimental data. Several excellent books in these areas already exist. Our aim has been to make some of the most important techniques accessible and useful to those who are just beginning their preparation for the scientific and engineering professions.

Acknowledgments

A preliminary version of the text has been read by sophomore physics students at Carnegie Institute of Technology under its original title, "Thirteen Short Mysteries." (The number of mysteries has since grown to sixteen.) The critical comments and suggestions of these students have helped considerably to clear up sections which were obscurely written. I am indebted to Professor Sir Ronald A. Fisher, Dr. Frank Yates, and to Messrs. Oliver & Boyd, Ltd., Edinburgh, for permission to reprint Tables IV and VI from their book "Statistical Tables for Biological, Agricultural and Medical Research." The very willing and cooperative assistance of Mrs. L. Horton, who typed several versions of the manuscript, is gratefully acknowledged. Particular thanks are due to Dr. Yardley Beers of the National Bureau of Standards, Prof. E. T. Jaynes of Washington University, Prof. Henry Margenau of Yale University, and Prof. Jay Orear of Cornell University. All these people have read the entire manuscript critically, and their comments and suggestions have resulted in substantial improvements in the text. Not all the suggestions have been followed, however; and responsibility for whatever shortcomings remain in the book rests entirely upon the author. The most important acknowledgment of all is on page v.

Hugh D. Young

CONTENTS

Contents

LIST OF SYMBOLS

The meanings of symbols which appear several times in the text are listed here for convenient reference.

A	normalization constant in a distribution function
$C(N, n)$	number of combinations of N things taken n at a time
D_μ	deviation of mean $\bar{x}_\mu$ from mean of means $\overline{X}$
M	number of sets of observations
N	number of observations in a set; number of independent events; parameter in binomial distribution
P	probability
P_i	probability of event i; probability for an observation to fall in interval i
Q	quantity calculated from observed quantities $a, b, \ldots$
T	multiple of standard deviation
$\overline{X}$	mean of means $\bar{x}_\mu$
Z	number of sets of observations or trials
a	parameter in Poisson distribution
$a, b, \ldots$	observed quantities
$a_i, b_i, \ldots$	typical observations of quantities $a, b, \ldots$
$\bar{a}, \bar{b}, \ldots$	mean values of quantities $a, b, \ldots$
b	y intercept in linear equation
b'	x intercept in linear equation

List of Symbols

d_i	deviation of observation i
$d_{\mu i}$	deviation of observation i in set μ
$f(n)$	function of n; probability distribution for discrete variable n
$f(x)$	function of x; probability distribution for continuous variable x
$f_a(n)$	Poisson distribution function
$f_{N,p}(n)$	binomial distribution function
$f'(x)$	derivative of $f(x)$
h	measure of precision in normal distribution
i	index to denote one of a set of observations
m	slope of line of regression of y on x
m'	slope of line of regression of x on y
p	parameter in binomial distribution
q	parameter in binomial distribution; $q = 1 - p$
r	linear correlation coefficient
w_i	weight of observation i
x	an observed quantity
x_i	typical observation of quantity x
$x_{\mu i}$	observation i in set μ of quantity x
$\bar{x}$	mean value of x; mean of observations x_i
$\bar{x}_\mu$	mean of set μ of observations
y	dependent variable in linear equation
$\Delta a, \Delta b, \ldots$	change in quantity $a, b, \ldots$
α	mean deviation, average deviation, average absolute deviation

ϵ	elemental error used to derive normal distribution
μ	index to denote a set of observations
ν	number of degrees of freedom
σ	standard deviation
σ^2	variance
σ_m	standard deviation of mean
σ_{ma}	standard deviation of mean of a
χ^2	measure of goodness of fit
$\cong$	approximately equal to
$\stackrel{\circ}{=}$	observed to be equal to

CHAPTER I

INTRODUCTION

In all branches of physical science and engineering, one deals constantly with numbers which result more or less directly from experimental observations. In fact, it can be said that the very essence of physical science is the discovering and the using of correlations among quantitative observations of physical phenomena.

Experimental observations always have inaccuracies. In using numbers which result from experimental observations, it is almost always necessary to know the extent of these inaccuracies. If several observations are used to compute a result, one must know how the inaccuracies of the individual observations contribute to the inaccuracy of the result. If one is comparing a number based on a theoretical prediction with one based on experiment, it is necessary to know something about the accuracies of both of these if one is to say anything intelligent about whether or not they agree. If one has some knowledge of the statistical behavior of errors of observation, it is often possible to reduce the effect of these uncertainties on the final result. Such problems as these will be discussed in the following pages.

1 | Kinds of Errors

In discussing errors in individual observations, it is customary to distinguish between *systematic* errors and *chance* or *random* errors.

Systematic errors are errors associated with the particular instruments or technique of measurement being used. Suppose we have a book which is 9 in. high. We measure its height by laying a ruler against it, with one end of the ruler at the top end of the book. If the first inch of the ruler has been previously cut off, then the ruler is likely to tell us that the book is 10 in. long. This is a *systematic* error. If a thermometer immersed in boiling pure water at normal pressure reads 102°C, it is improperly calibrated. If readings from this thermometer are incorporated into experimental results, a systematic error results. An ammeter which is not properly "zeroed" introduces a systematic error.

Very often, in experimental work, systematic errors are more important than chance errors. They are also, however, much more difficult to deal with. There are no general principles for avoiding systematic errors; only an experimenter whose skill has come through long experience can consistently detect systematic errors and prevent or correct them.

Random errors are produced by a large number of unpredictable and unknown variations in the experimental situation. They can result from small errors in judgment on the part of the observer, such as in estimating tenths of the smallest scale division. Other causes are unpredictable fluctuations in conditions, such as temperature, illumination, line voltage, or any kind of mechanical vibrations of the equipment. It is found empirically that such random errors are frequently distributed according to a simple law. This makes it possible to use statistical methods to deal with random errors. This statistical treatment will form the principal body of the following discussion.

There is a third class, containing what are sometimes called errors but which are not, properly speaking, errors at all. These include mistakes in recording numbers, blunders of reading instruments incorrectly, and mistakes in arithmetic. These types of inaccuracies have no place in a well-done experiment. They can always be eliminated completely by careful work.

The terms *accuracy* and *precision* are often used to distinguish between systematic and random errors. If a measurement has small *systematic* errors, we say that it has high *accuracy;* if small *random* errors, we say it has high *precision*.

2 | Propagation of Errors

Propagation of errors is nothing but a fancy way of describing the obvious fact that if one uses various experimental observations to calculate a result, and if the observations have errors associated with them, then the result will also be in error by an amount which depends on the errors of the individual observations.

Ordinarily it is not possible to calculate directly the errors in the results, because the errors in the observations are not usually known. If we knew them, we could correct the observations and eliminate the errors! The results of this section are thus not directly useful for treating propagation of experimental errors, but they can be used to obtain formulas which are useful. This will be the principal task of Sec. 13. Meanwhile, the results obtained in this section are directly useful in cases where the "error" is not really an error but a small change in the value of a known quantity, and we want to compute the effect which this change has on the result of a calculation which contains this quantity.

For example, suppose one wants to determine the volume of a cylinder by measuring its radius r and its height h, using the formula

$$V = \pi r^2 h \tag{2.1}$$

There may be an error in the measurement of r, so that the result of our measurement is not r but something slightly different, say $r + \Delta r$ (where Δr is the error). If there is a similar error Δh in measuring the height, then our result is not V, the true value, but something slightly different, $V + \Delta V$. We can calculate ΔV as follows. In the formula we place $r + \Delta r$ instead of just r and $h + \Delta h$ instead of h; then the result is $V + \Delta V$:

$$V + \Delta V = \pi(r + \Delta r)^2(h + \Delta h) \tag{2.2}$$

If we expand this, and subtract V from both sides of the equation, the result is

$$\Delta V = \pi(r^2\, \Delta h + 2rh\, \Delta r + \Delta r^2 h + 2r\, \Delta r\, \Delta h + \Delta r^2\, \Delta h)$$
$$(2.3)$$

Now if the error Δr is much smaller than r itself, and if

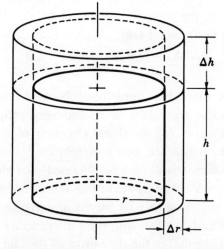

Fig. 2.1. Changes in the volume of a cylinder resulting from changes Δr and Δh in its dimensions. Can you identify the separate terms of Eq. (2.4) in the figure?

Δh is much smaller than h, the last three terms in Eq. (2.3) are much smaller than the first two; hence we can write approximately

$$\Delta V \cong \pi(r^2\, \Delta h + 2rh\, \Delta r) \qquad (2.4)$$

which allows us to calculate the error ΔV if we know r, h, and their errors. Describing this result in different words, we may say that Eq. (2.4) gives a means of calculating how much the volume of a cylinder changes if we change its dimensions by the amounts Δr and Δh.

Often we are interested not in the error itself, but in the so-called fractional error, which is defined as the *ratio* of the error of the quantity to the true value of the quantity; in the present case this is $\Delta V/V$. Using Eqs. (2.1) and (2.4), we obtain

$$\frac{\Delta V}{V} \simeq \frac{\pi(r^2\,\Delta h + 2rh\,\Delta r)}{\pi r^2 h} = \frac{\Delta h}{h} + \frac{2\Delta r}{r} \qquad (2.5)$$

This is a remarkably simple result because it shows that the fractional error in V is related very simply to the fractional errors (or fractional changes) of the quantities h and r which are used to determine V.

This same result can be obtained in a slightly different way. We can approximate the error in V resulting from the error in r by means of derivatives. If the errors ΔV and Δr are small, then the ratio $\Delta V/\Delta r$ is approximately equal to the derivative dV/dr. But $dV/dr = 2\pi rh$. Hence, we have approximately

$$\frac{\Delta V}{\Delta r} \simeq 2\pi rh \quad \text{and} \quad \frac{\Delta V}{V} \simeq \frac{2\pi rh\,\Delta r}{\pi r^2 h} = 2\,\frac{\Delta r}{r} \quad (2.6)$$

This gives the part of the fractional error in V which results from the error in r. A similar calculation gives the contribution of Δh, and the total fractional error $\Delta V/V$ is the same as obtained previously.

Because V is a function of both r and h, the correct mathematical language for the derivative of V with respect to r which we have used above is $\partial V/\partial r$, which is read "partial derivative of V with respect to r," and means simply that we recognize that V is a function of other variables besides r, but we are evaluating the derivative with respect to r, while all the other variables are kept constant. Similarly, we can define a partial derivative of V with respect to h, $\partial V/\partial h$. An approximate expression for the error ΔV can then be written:

$$\Delta V \cong \frac{\partial V}{\partial r} \Delta r + \frac{\partial V}{\partial h} \Delta h \tag{2.7}$$

Let us generalize this result. Suppose we have a quantity Q which depends upon several observed quantities $a, b, c, \ldots$. The error ΔQ resulting from errors Δa, $\Delta b, \ldots$ can be represented as

$$\Delta Q = \frac{\partial Q}{\partial a} \Delta a + \frac{\partial Q}{\partial b} \Delta b + \frac{\partial Q}{\partial c} \Delta c + \cdots \tag{2.8}$$

and the fractional error $\Delta Q/Q$ as

$$\frac{\Delta Q}{Q} = \frac{1}{Q} \frac{\partial Q}{\partial a} \Delta a + \frac{1}{Q} \frac{\partial Q}{\partial b} \Delta b + \cdots \tag{2.9}$$

As was mentioned at the beginning of this section, the discussion just given is not of much direct usefulness in the analysis of propagation of errors. We have talked as though we knew the true values of the observed quantities, along with the errors in the observations. In some particular cases this may be true; or we may want to compute the change in Q which results from given values of $a, b, \ldots$. Then we may use Eq. (2.8).

But often this is not the case. Ordinarily we do

not know the errors exactly because errors usually occur randomly. Often the *distribution* of errors in a set
of observations is known, but the error in any individual observation is not known. Later, after acquiring
some fundamental knowledge of statistical methods, we
shall learn in Sec. 13 some considerably more sophisti-
cated methods for treating problems in propagation of
errors. The methods of Sec. 13 will be of much greater
practical usefulness than the naïve considerations given
in this section.

Another consideration is that it is not always clear
whether or not such a thing as a "true value" really
exists. Suppose we are trying to measure the length of
a broken stick, whose ends are uneven and jagged. We
may be able to state that the length is between certain
limits, say between 14 and 15 in. But if we try to be
more precise we have to decide where the ends are; if
we aspire to measure the length to within 0.01 in., we
cannot say that to this precision the stick *has* a definite
length.

In most of what follows, we shall assume that we
are making measurements on quantities for which true
values really exist. We should keep in mind, however,
that there are areas of physics in which it is not correct
to say that a particular observable quantity *has* a definite
value. This basic uncertainty of some basic physical
quantities is, in fact, one of the fundamental notions of
quantum mechanics. In quantum-mechanical problems

one must often be content with the statement that the *average* of a large number of observations has a definite value.

3 | The Mean and Dispersion

Suppose we want to make an accurate measurement of the diameter of a hard steel rod with a micrometer caliper. Assuming that the rod *has* a "true diameter," we will probably get several different results if we make the measurement several times. We may tighten the micrometer more sometimes than others, there may be small dust particles present, we may make small errors in estimating tenths of the smallest scale division, etc. Still, one suspects intuitively that it should be possible to obtain a more reliable result for the diameter by using the 10 measurements than by using only one measurement.

What then shall we do with the 10 measurements? The first procedure which obviously suggests itself is simply to take the *average*, or arithmetic *mean*. The *mean* of a set of numbers is defined as the sum of all the numbers divided by the number of them. If we have 10 measurements we add them all up and divide by 10. In a more general language which we shall use often, let us call a typical observation x_i. If there are 10 observations, then the index i can have any value from 1 to 10. If there are N observations, then i ranges from 1 to N.

In general, we may define the mean $\bar{x}$ of the set of numbers x_i as

$$\bar{x} = \frac{x_1 + x_2 + \cdots + x_{N-1} + x_N}{N} \tag{3.1}$$

In what follows, a bar over a letter will always signify a "mean value." A convenient mathematical shorthand which we frequently use is

$$\bar{x} = \frac{1}{N} \sum_{i=1}^{N} x_i \tag{3.2}$$

In this expression, the symbol

$$\sum_{i=1}^{N}$$

is read "the sum from $i = 1$ to N"; its meaning is that in the expression which follows Σ we first place $i = 1$, add to it the result of placing $i = 2$ and so on, up to $i = N$, which is the last value of i. Thus,

$$\sum_{i=1}^{N} x_i = x_1 + x_2 + x_3 + \cdots + x_{N-1} + x_N$$

It will be seen later that in some important cases there is a good reason for regarding the *average* of a set of measurements as the *best* estimate of the true value of the quantity being measured. For the present, however, we observe simply that taking the average seems intuitively to be a reasonable procedure.

Sometimes we want to compute the mean of a set of numbers (which may be measurements or anything else) in which we think that some numbers are more important than others. How shall we make the calculation? If, for example, two observers guess the height of a tree as 30 and 60 ft, respectively, and we have twice as much confidence in the first observer as the second, how shall we compute a combined "best guess" as to the height of the tree?

A procedure which immediately suggests itself is to

Fig. 3.1. Observations with unequal weights.

pretend that the 30-ft guess was made more than once. Suppose, for example, we include it in the average twice. Then, of course, we must divide by the total number of guesses, which is now three. Then our best guess will be

$$\frac{2(30 \text{ ft}) + 1(60 \text{ ft})}{2 + 1} = 40 \text{ ft}$$

More generally, if we have several guesses with different degrees of reliability, we can multiply each by an appropriate weighting factor, and then divide the sum of these products by the sum of all the weighting factors.

Such considerations lead us to the idea of a *weighted mean*. The weighted mean of a set of numbers is defined as follows: For each number x_i in the set $(x_1, x_2, \ldots, x_N)$ we assign a weighting factor, or weight w_i. The weighted mean $\bar{x}$ is then defined as

$$\bar{x} = \frac{w_1 x_1 + w_2 x_2 + \cdots + w_N x_N}{w_1 + w_2 + \cdots + w_N} = \frac{\displaystyle\sum_{i=1}^{N} w_i x_i}{\displaystyle\sum_{i=1}^{N} w_i} \qquad (3.3)$$

Note that if all the weights are unity (or, more generally, if they are all equal) the weighted mean reduces to the mean as previously defined by Eq. (3.2).

Having obtained a set of measurements x_i and the mean $\bar{x}$, we should like to have a way of stating quantitatively how much the individual measurements are scattered away from the mean. A quantitative description of the *scatter* (or *spread* or *dispersion*) of the measurements will give us some idea of the precision of these measurements.

To obtain such a quantitative description, we first define a deviation d_i for each measurement x_i. The deviation d_i is defined as the difference between any measurement x_i and the mean $\bar{x}$ of the set. That is,

$$d_i = x_i - \bar{x} \qquad (3.4)$$

(We could equally well have defined d_i as $\bar{x} - x_i$ instead of $x_i - \bar{x}$; the definition given here is the conventional one. Some authors refer to the d_i as *residuals* rather than deviations. The two terms are synonymous.)

It should be noted here that it would *not* be correct to call d_i the *error* in measurement x_i, because $\bar{x}$ is not actually the true value of the observed quantity. It can be shown that in many cases, if a very large number of observations is made, $\bar{x}$ *approaches* the true value of the quantity (assuming that there are no systematic errors), and then the deviations d_i *approach* the true errors in the measurements x_i. This is the case, for example, if the errors are distributed according to the Gauss distribution, or "normal error function," to be discussed in Sec. 9.

As a first attempt at a quantitative description of the spread or dispersion of the measurements x_i about the mean, we might consider the average of the deviations. This is

$$\frac{1}{N} \sum_{i=1}^{N} d_i = \frac{1}{N} \sum_{i=1}^{N} (x_i - \bar{x}) \tag{3.5}$$

The right-hand side of Eq. (3.5) is a sum of N terms, each one of which is itself a sum of two terms. The order of adding these terms is immaterial; so we could just as well add all the first terms, then add all the second terms; that is,

$$\frac{1}{N} \sum_{i=1}^{N} (x_i - \bar{x}) = \frac{1}{N} \left(\sum_{i=1}^{N} x_i - \sum_{i=1}^{N} \bar{x} \right) \tag{3.6}$$

Now what is the meaning of the second term on the

13

right side of Eq. (3.6)? It is a sum of N terms, but they are all the same. We simply add $\bar{x}$ itself N times. That is,

$$\sum_{i=1}^{N} \bar{x} = N\bar{x}$$

Thus the expression for the average of the residuals boils down to

$$\frac{1}{N} \sum_{i=1}^{N} d_i = \frac{1}{N} \sum_{i=1}^{N} (x_i - \bar{x}) = \frac{1}{N} \sum_{i=1}^{N} x_i - \bar{x} = 0$$

(3.7)

because of Eq. (3.2). The average of the residuals is always zero.

This should not be particularly surprising; some of the observations are larger than the mean, and some are smaller than the mean; so some of the residuals are positive, and some are negative. Because of the way we define the average and the residuals, the *average* of the residuals is *always* zero. This means that the average of the residuals is not very useful as a characterization of the scatter or dispersion.

Perhaps a better idea would be to take the absolute value of each residual and average the absolute values. We thereby obtain what is called the *mean deviation*, denoted by α. That is,

$$\alpha = \frac{1}{N} \sum_{i=1}^{N} |d_i| = \frac{1}{N} \sum_{i=1}^{N} |x_i - \bar{x}|$$

(3.8)

This quantity is often referred to as the average deviation; this is a misnomer, as is "mean deviation." It is not the average deviation but the average of the *absolute values* of the deviations. This quantity is sometimes used to characterize the spread or dispersion of the measurements. For various reasons which will be discussed later, it is not so useful as another one which will be defined next, called *standard deviation.*

In defining the standard deviation, we get around the problem of handling the negative residuals by *squaring* each deviation, thereby obtaining a quantity which is always positive. We then take the *average* of the *squares*, and then take the *square root* of this result. Thus the standard deviation can also be referred to as the *root-mean-square deviation*, in that it is the square root of the mean of the squares of the deviations. The standard deviation is usually symbolized by σ, and its defining equation is

$$\sigma = \sqrt{\frac{1}{N} \sum_{i=1}^{N} d_i^2} = \sqrt{\frac{1}{N} \sum_{i=1}^{N} (x_i - \bar{x})^2} \tag{3.9}$$

The square of the standard deviation σ^2 is called the *variance* of the set of observations. Note that σ always has the same units as the x_i, and that it is always positive.

One might now ask, How is σ related to the precision of the *mean*, $\bar{x}$? Clearly, it is unlikely that $\bar{x}$ is in error by as much as σ if the number of observations is large. It will be shown in Sec. 12 that in many cases the error in $\bar{x}$ is not likely to be greater than $\sigma/N^{1/2}$. Thus, as we should expect, more measurements give a more reliable mean.

We now transform Eq. (3.9), which defines σ, into another form which involves only the observations x_i. This new form will not be particularly useful, except perhaps for machine calculations; but it provides us with an excuse for doing some more manipulations with summation symbols similar to the manipulations used in showing that the average of the deviations is zero.

We square the entire expression, and then multiply out the squared term following Σ:

$$\sigma^2 = \frac{1}{N} \sum (x_i - \bar{x})^2 = \frac{1}{N} \sum (x_i{}^2 - 2x_i\bar{x} + \bar{x}^2) \quad (3.10)$$

In this expression and those which follow, we drop the limits on the summation symbol in order to save writing. Unless otherwise noted, we assume that the summation runs over the number of measurements, that is, from $i = 1$ to N. Now, as before, we separate the various terms in the sum:

$$\sigma^2 = \frac{1}{N} \sum x_i{}^2 - \frac{1}{N} \sum 2x_i\bar{x} + \frac{1}{N} \sum \bar{x}^2 \quad (3.11)$$

The second term in Eq. (3.11) is a sum in which every term contains the quantity $2\bar{x}$ as a factor. It is therefore legitimate to factor out $2\bar{x}$ and write this term as

$$-\frac{1}{N} \sum 2x_i\bar{x} = -\frac{1}{N} (2\bar{x}) \sum x_i = -2\bar{x}^2 \quad (3.12)$$

where we have used the definition of the mean, Eq. (3.2). Furthermore, the third term of Eq. (3.11) contains a sum of N terms, each of which is just $\bar{x}^2$; so the value of the term is just $\bar{x}^2$. Therefore the whole expression can be written:

$$\sigma^2 = \frac{1}{N} \sum x_i{}^2 - \bar{x}^2 = \frac{1}{N} \sum x_i{}^2 - \left(\frac{1}{N} \sum x_i\right)^2 \quad (3.13)$$

It is important to note that in general the quantities $\Sigma(x_i{}^2)$ and $(\Sigma x_i)^2$ are not equal; if you do not believe this, try writing out some terms of each of these sums.

The following is an example which illustrates the calculation of the mean, the average absolute deviation, and the standard deviation of a set of observations. Here $N = 6$.

i	x_i, in.	d_i, in.	$d_i{}^2$, in.^{2}
1	0.251	0.001	0.000001
2	0.248	-0.002	0.000004
3	0.250	0.000	0.000000
4	0.249	-0.001	0.000001
5	0.250	0.000	0.000000
6	0.252	0.002	0.000004
	$\Sigma x_i = 1.500$ in.	$\Sigma |d_i| = 0.006$ in.	$\Sigma d_i{}^2 = 0.000010$ in.^{2}
	$\bar{x} = \frac{1}{6} \Sigma x_i$	$\alpha = \frac{1}{6} \Sigma |d_i|$	$\sigma = \sqrt{\frac{1}{6} \Sigma d_i{}^2}$
	$= 0.2500$ in.	$= 0.001$ in.	$= 0.0013$ in.

In analogy to the fractional errors defined in Sec. 2, we sometimes use the *fractional standard deviation*, defined as the ratio of the standard deviation to the mean $\sigma/\bar{x}$ or the *per cent standard deviation* $(\sigma/\bar{x}) \times 100\%$. In the previous example, the fractional standard deviation is

0.0013 in./0.250 in. = 0.005, and the per cent standard deviation is 0.5%. Note that the fractional standard deviation is always a pure number (without units) because it is always a ratio of two numbers with the same units.

If a weighted mean of the numbers x_i, with weights w_i, has been computed, then the definitions of the mean deviation and standard deviation should be modified somewhat. We shall postpone until later a detailed discussion of how to calculate the standard deviation of a weighted mean. This discussion will be made easier by use of the concept of standard deviation of the mean introduced in Sec. 12 and the analysis of propagation of errors in Sec. 13. By the time we reach these sections, we shall also have some techniques for assigning weights to numbers, in a few situations of practical importance.

PROBLEMS

1. The numerical value of e, the base of natural logarithms, is approximately

$e = 2.7182\ 8182\ 8459\ 0452\ 3536$

An infinite series which can be used to compute this value is

$e = 1 + 1/1 + 1/1 \cdot 2 + 1/1 \cdot 2 \cdot 3 + 1/1 \cdot 2 \cdot 3 \cdot 4 + \cdots$

Find the fractional error which results from taking the following:

a. The first three terms of the series.

b. The first five terms.

2. The numerical value of π is approximately

$$\pi = 3.1415\ 9265\ 3589\ 7932\ 3846$$

Find the fractional error in the following approximate values:

a. $^{22}/_7$.

b. $^{355}/_{113}$.

3. An inaccurate automobile speedometer reads 65 mph when the true speed is 60 mph, and 90 mph when the true speed is 80 mph. Does the fractional error increase or decrease with increasing speed?

4. In Prob. 3, suppose that the error changes proportionately with the speed. At what speed will there be zero error? Is the result the same if instead the *fractional error* is assumed to change proportionately with speed?

5. A certain automobile engine has pistons 3.000 in. in diameter. By approximately what fraction is the piston displacement increased if the cylinder bore (diameter) is increased to 3.060 in. and oversize pistons are installed?

6. A certain type of paper used for stationery is referred to as "twenty pound" because a ream (500 sheets) of 17- by 22-in. sheets weighs 20 lb. If the sheets are $\frac{1}{16}$ in. oversize in each dimension, how much will a ream weigh?

7. If the mass of a stationary particle is m_0, its apparent mass when moving with velocity v is given by relativity theory as $m = m_0(1 - v^2/c^2)^{-1/2}$, where c is the velocity of light, $c = 3 \times 10^8$ m/sec. By what fraction does the mass of an electron differ from its rest mass if its velocity is:

a. 3×10^4 m/sec?

b. 3×10^7 m/sec?

8. It is often convenient to approximate powers of numbers close to unity by using the binomial theorem. For example,

$$(1.01)^2 = (1 + 0.01)^2 = 1 + 2(0.01) + (0.01)^2$$
$$= 1 + 0.02 + 0.0001$$
$$\cong 1.02$$

The error in this approximation is $0.0001/1.0201 \cong 0.01\%$. Show that, in general, if $\delta \ll 1$, then $(1 + \delta)^n \cong 1 + n\delta$, and that the *error* in this approximation is about $\frac{1}{2}n(n - 1)\delta^2$.

9. Use the results of Prob. 8 to obtain the approximation $(A + \delta)^n \cong A^n + n\delta A^{n-1}$, valid when $\delta \ll A$. What is the fractional error in this approximation?

10. Use the method of Prob. 8 to find approximately the values of:

    a. $(1.001)^3$

    b. $1/0.998$

    c. $\sqrt{1.004}$

11. Two lengths a and b are measured with a meter stick, with a possible error of 0.1 cm in each. The values obtained are

    $a = 50.0$ cm $b = 55.0$ cm

    a. What is the maximum error in the quantity $(a + b)$? In $(a - b)$?

    b. What is the maximum fractional error in $(a + b)$? In $(a - b)$?

12. In a "tangent galvanometer," the current is proportional to the tangent of the angle of deflection of the galvanometer needle. That is, $I = C \tan \theta$. If the error in measuring θ is known, find the value of θ for which:

    a. The error in I is smallest.

    b. The fractional error in I is smallest.

13. The acceleration of gravity g can be obtained by measuring the period T of a simple pendulum and its length l, using the relation $T = 2\pi\sqrt{l/g}$. Suppose the period was

observed to be 2 sec, with an error of observation of 0.02 sec, and the length was observed to be 1 m, with an error of observation of 0.01 m.

a. What is the maximum error in *g*? The minimum error?

b. Which of the errors contributes most to the error in *g*? Why?

14. The components F_x and F_y of a vector with length F, making an angle θ with the positive x axis in an x-y coordinate system, are given by

$$F_x = F \cos \theta \qquad F_y = F \sin \theta$$

If an error $\Delta\theta$ is made in the measurement of θ, derive expressions for the errors and fractional errors in F_x and F_y.

15. Approximately what fractional errors might be expected in the following measurements:

a. A distance of 10 cm measured with an ordinary meter stick.

b. A mass of 1 g measured with an analytical balance.

c. A ¼-in. steel rod measured with a good micrometer caliper.

d. A human hair measured with a good micrometer caliper.

e. A voltage of 1.5 volts measured with a meter having a scale 3 in. long with full-scale reading 5 volts.

16. Find the mean, standard deviation, and mean deviation of the following set of numbers:

1, 2, 3, 4, 5

17. For the set of numbers (1, 2, 3, 4, 5, 6) find:

a. The mean.

b. The weighted mean in which the weights are 1, 1, 2, 2, 3, 3, respectively.

  c. The weighted mean in which the weights are 1, 2, 3, 3, 2, 1, respectively.

  18. Ten measurements of the diameter of a hard steel rod with a micrometer caliper yielded the following data:

Diameter, in.

0.250	0.246
0.252	0.250
0.255	0.248
0.249	0.250
0.248	0.252

Calculate the standard deviation and mean deviation of this set of measurements.

  19. Show that the error in the *mean* of a series of measurements is always smaller than the largest error in an individual measurement.

  20. In a certain set of observations, one observation has a much larger deviation from the mean than the others. If this observation is omitted from the calculations, which measure of spread is affected more, the mean deviation or the standard deviation? Why?

  21. If the mean of a large set of observations is *m*, and all deviations between $-e$ and $+e$ occur equally often, find the mean deviation and standard deviation.

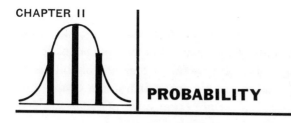

CHAPTER II

PROBABILITY

Any quantitative analysis of random errors of observation must be based on probability theory. It is instructive to consider some simple probability calculations first, as preparation for the task of applying probability theory to the study of random errors.

4 | The Meaning of Probability

If we throw a penny up in the air, we know intuitively that the "chance" of its coming down heads is one-half, or 50%. If we roll an ordinary die (singular of dice) we know that the chance of the number 5 coming up is one-sixth.

What does this really mean, though? On each flip of the penny it comes down either heads or tails; there is no such thing as a penny coming down half heads and half tails. What we really mean is that if we flip the penny a very large number of times, the number of times it comes down heads will be approximately one-half the total number of trials. And, if we roll one die

23

a very large number of times, the number 5 will come up on one-sixth of the trials. For our purposes, it will almost always be most useful to define probabilities in this way. That is, we ask in what fraction of the total number of trials a certain event takes place, if we make a very large number of trials.[1]

It should be pointed out that in the penny-flipping problem we have stated only that the *ratio* of the number of heads to the total number of trials approaches the value one-half as the number of trials becomes very large. This is not the same thing as saying that the *number* of heads approaches the *number* of tails. For example, for 100 flips a fairly probable result is 52 heads. For 10,000 flips a fairly probable result is 5020 heads. In this second case the ratio is much closer to one-half than in the first; yet the *differences* between the number of heads and the number of tails is larger. As a matter of fact, it can be shown that the difference between the number of heads and the number of tails is likely to become very large despite the fact that the ratio of each to the total number of trials approaches one-half. So if you are matching pennies with someone and are losing, you cannot necessarily expect to regain your losses after a sufficiently large number of trials. There is a 50%

[1] A very lucid discussion of some of the basic concepts of probability theory is found in Lindsay and Margenau, "Foundations of Physics," chapter IV, which is available in an inexpensive paperback Dover edition. Many other chapters of this book are also very useful in clarifying some of the basic concepts of physics.

chance that you will lose more and more. But, enough of moralizing.

If we know the probabilities for some simple events, such as tossing a coin or rolling a die, we can calculate probabilities for more complicated events which are composed of these simple events. For example, suppose we flip two pennies at the same time and ask for the probability of getting one head and one tail. When two pennies are flipped, each one can come down in two ways with equal probabilities, so that for two pennies there are four possibilities all together: two heads; heads on the first, tails on the second; tails on the first, heads on the second; or both tails. All four of these possibilities are equally likely, so that we say that each one has a probability ¼. Of the four, two have what we are looking for, namely, one head and one tail. Therefore, the probability of one head and one tail is ½. The probability of two heads is of course ¼, as is the probability of two tails.

Note that these probabilities are always numbers less than 1. If we *add* all the probabilities for *all* the events that can possibly happen, we obtain the total probability that something will happen, which is of course unity.

Here is a slightly more complicated problem. Suppose we roll two dice, the classical number. We ask: What is the probability of rolling 7? Now each die can come down in six positions; so for the two dice there are 36 possible results of rolling two dice, all equally likely. (If we roll n dice, the number of different possibilities is 6^n.) How many of these add up to 7? It is convenient to tabulate the possibilities:

Die 1	Die 2
1	6
2	5
3	4
4	3
5	2
6	1

Thus, there are six ways of getting 7 with two dice; the probability for each is $\frac{1}{36}$. The probability of rolling 7 is therefore $\frac{6}{36}$, or $\frac{1}{6}$. In exactly the same way one can show that the probability for 11 is $\frac{2}{36}$, or $\frac{1}{18}$. The probability of rolling either 7 or 11 is the sum of these, $\frac{8}{36}$ or $\frac{2}{9}$, a fact which you may already know.

Note that in the above example, if any of several different events can be regarded as a success, the *total* probability of success is simply the *sum* of the probabilities of the individual events. The situation is a little different if more than one requirement is to be satisfied in order to make the event a success. Suppose, for some strange reason, we rolled two dice and a penny and asked for the probability that the dice will come up totaling 7 and the penny will come up heads. We can look at this problem in two ways. One way is to say that we now have twice as many possibilities as previously because for each of the 36 dice positions there are two positions of the coin, so that we have 72 equally likely

26

possibilities in all. Still only six of these are favorable; so we say that the probability of success is $\frac{6}{72}$, or $\frac{1}{12}$.

The other, and equally valid, point of view is to recall that the dice rolling and the penny tossing are independent events, each with its own probability. The probability that the dice will come up totaling 7 is $\frac{1}{6}$; the probability that the coin will come up heads is one-half. The probability that *both* these things will happen at the same time is the product of the two probabilities, or $\frac{1}{12}$, in agreement with our other result.

In general, if we are considering several separate and independent events, each with its own probability, the probability that *all* the events will occur is the *product* of the individual probabilities. This fact operates to the advantage of railroads, for example. The probability that a railroad engineer will fall asleep is a small number. The probability that the automatic block-signal system will fail is some other small number. But, for a wreck to take place, both of these things would have to take place at once, and the probability that *both* the engineer will fall asleep *and* the signal system will fail is the product of the two small numbers and is therefore a much smaller number.

To conclude this section, here is another problem of probabilities. Every book concerned with probability contains at least one problem involving drawing black balls and white balls out of an urn; there is no reason why this book should be an exception.

The particular urn we have in mind contains six

white balls and four black ones. They cannot be distinguished by touch, and we draw them out without looking. If two balls are drawn out, what is the probability that one is white and the other black, if the first is not replaced before the second is drawn?

Clearly there are two possibilities which we should call successes: white on the first draw and black on the second, and the reverse. Considering the first possibility, we need to multiply the probability of a white ball on the first draw, which is $\frac{6}{10}$, by the probability of a black ball on the second, which is not $\frac{4}{10}$, but $\frac{4}{9}$, since after the first draw the number remaining is 9, of which 4 are black. Thus, the probability of white on the first and black on the second is $(\frac{6}{10})(\frac{4}{9}) = \frac{24}{90} = \frac{4}{15}$. Similarly, the probability of black on the first and white on the second is $(\frac{4}{10})(\frac{6}{9}) = \frac{24}{90} = \frac{4}{15}$. The sum of these gives the probability for one white ball and one black one, in either order. This is $\frac{4}{15} + \frac{4}{15} = \frac{8}{15}$.

The result would have been different if we had replaced the first draw. Then the probability for each case would have been $(\frac{6}{10})(\frac{4}{10}) = \frac{24}{100} = \frac{6}{25}$, so that the total probability would be $\frac{12}{25}$. Making up more problems as we go along, we note that the probability for two blacks is $(\frac{4}{10})(\frac{3}{9})$ if the first ball is not replaced, since after the first draw only three blacks are left if the first ball was black. If the first draw is replaced, then the probability is $(\frac{4}{10})(\frac{4}{10})$. And so on.

5 | Permutations and Combinations

The probability calculations in some complicated problems which we will encounter are facilitated considerably

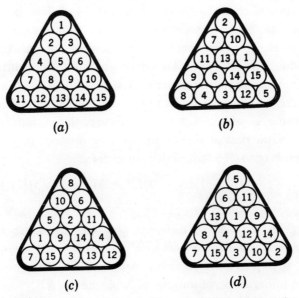

Fig. 5.1. A few of the possible permutations of 15 pool balls. The total number of possible permutations is 15! = 1,307,674,368,000.

by the use of the ideas of permutations and combinations, which we now introduce.

We consider first the idea of permutations of a set of objects. A set of pool balls consists of 15 balls, numbered from 1 to 15. These can be placed in the rack in a number of different ways, not all of which are legal.

In how many different ways can the balls be arranged? Suppose we also number the positions in the rack from 1 to 15, and fill these positions one at a time. To fill the first position we have our choice of any of the 15 balls. For each of these 15 choices there are 14 choices for the second position, because there are 14 balls remaining. For each of these there are 13 choices for the next position, and so forth. Therefore, the number of different ways of filling the entire rack is $(15)(14)(13)(12) \cdots (3)(2)(1)$. Do not bother to multiply out this product; its value is about 1.3×10^{12}, a very large number. The mathematical shorthand for this product is $(15!)$, which is read "15 factorial." In general,

$$N! = N(N - 1)(N - 2)(N - 3) \cdots (4)(3)(2)(1)$$

$$(5.1)$$

The number of different ways of arranging the 15 objects is called the *number of permutations of* 15 *objects*, and as we have shown this is equal to 15!. In general, the number of permutations of N objects is $(N!)$.

Next, we consider a slightly different problem, that of selecting a certain number of objects from a group containing a larger number. Let us start with an example. Consider a club containing a total of 10 members. From these members a committee consisting of four members is to be selected. How many different committees can we find?

We can start by choosing one of the 10 members as the first one on the committee; then there are 9 left to choose for the second member, 8 for the third, and 7 for the fourth. Thus, we might be tempted to say that the total number of possibilities is $(10)(9)(8)(7)$. This, however, is not correct. The reason is that a number of these possibilities would have the same four people, but chosen in various orders. Since we do not care in what order the people are chosen, we do not

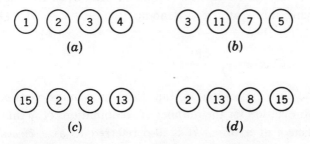

(a)   *(b)*

(c)   *(d)*

Fig. 5.2. A few of the possible combinations of 15 pool balls taken four at a time. Arrangements (c) and (d) contain the same balls in different orders; hence they are the *same* combination. The total number of distinct combinations is $15!/11!\ 4! = 1365$.

want to count these as different possibilities. Therefore, we must *divide* the above number by the number of ways of rearranging four people, which is simply the number of *permutations* of four objects, 4!. The correct result for the number of four-man committees which can be chosen from a group of 10 people, if the order of choice is irrelevant, is $(10)(9)(8)(7)/(4)(3)(2)(1)$. This is known as the *number of combinations of 10 objects taken four at a time*.

In general, the number of combinations of N things taken n at a time, which we abbreviate $C(N,n)$, is

$$C(N,n) = \frac{N(N-1)(N-2)\cdots(N-n+2)(N-n+1)}{n!}$$

$$(5.2)$$

This expression can be simplified somewhat by multiplying numerator and denominator by $(N-n)!$. The result is then

$$C(N,n) = \frac{N!}{(N-n)!\,n!} = \binom{N}{n} \tag{5.3}$$

The last expression in Eq. (5.3) is a more common abbreviation for the number of combinations of N things taken n at a time. It is also referred to as a *binomial coefficient*, for reasons which will be explained. From now on, we shall use the notation

$$\binom{N}{n}$$

rather than $C(N,n)$.

In Eq. (5.3) and in other places, we will sometimes encounter cases where $(0!)$ appears, and this has not been defined. How shall we define $(0!)$? The number of combinations of N things taken all N at a time (which is of course just 1) is given by

$$C(N,N) = \binom{N}{N} = \frac{N!}{0!\,N!} = \frac{1}{0!} \tag{5.4}$$

Thus, Eq. (5.3) is correct in all cases only if $0! = 1$. This is in fact reasonable if we regard 0! not as containing a factor zero, but as containing *no factors at all*, so that $0! \times 1 = 1$. We therefore agree on the definition

$$0! = 1 \tag{5.5}$$

The binomial coefficients are, as the name implies, closely related to the binomial theorem. To illustrate the relationship, we consider first a particular example, the expansion of

$$(a + b)^3 = (a + b)(a + b)(a + b)$$

When these three factors are multiplied out, there are terms of the form a^3, a^2b, ab^2, and b^3. The problem is to find the coefficient of each of these terms. First, we note that the only way the term a^3 can appear is from the product in which the factor a is taken in all three of the parentheses. The term a^2b arises from taking a in any two parentheses and b in the third; the number of times this term appears will therefore be the number of different ways that two factors a can be selected from the three parentheses, namely, the number of combinations of three things taken two at a time, which is $3!/2!\,1! = 3$. We therefore find

$$(a + b)^3 = a^3 + 3a^2b + 3ab^2 + b^3$$

More generally, in expanding a binomial $(a + b)^N$, we note that the expansion is a sum of terms all of which have the form $a^{N-n}b^n$, where n ranges from 0 to N. The number of times this term appears in the expansion is again just the number of combinations of N objects taken n at a time, the "objects" in this case being the b terms in the expansion. We therefore conclude

$$(a + b)^N = \sum_{n=0}^{N} \binom{N}{n} a^{N-n} b^n = \sum_{n=0}^{N} \frac{N!}{(N - n)!\, n!} a^{N-n} b^n$$

(5.6)

which is a fancy way of writing the old familiar binomial theorem.

A useful formula for the sum of a set of binomial coefficients can be obtained by placing $a = 1$ and $b = 1$ in this equation. The result is

$$(1 + 1)^N = 2^N = \sum_{n=0}^{N} \binom{N}{n}$$

(5.7)

This may not look particularly useful now, but its usefulness will appear soon.

PROBLEMS

1. A bag contains 10 white marbles and 10 black ones. If three marbles are drawn without looking, what is the probability that all three will be black? Is the situation different if each marble is replaced before the next is drawn?

2. In the game of Russian roulette (not recommended) one inserts one cartridge in a revolver whose capacity is six, spins the chamber, aims at one's head, and pulls the trigger. What is the chance of still being alive after playing the game:

    a. Once?

    b. Twice?

c. Three times?

d. A very large number of times?

3. A special pair of dice are marked in the following unorthodox manner: Each die has 1 on three faces, 2 on two faces, and 3 on the remaining face. Find the probabilities for all possible totals when the dice are rolled.

4. Consider a die which, instead of being cubical, is in the shape of a regular tetrahedron (four faces, all equilateral triangles) with numbers 1 to 4. If three such dice are rolled, find the probabilities for all possible totals. Represent the results on a graph.

5. In a group of 30 people selected at random, what is the probability that at least two have the same birthday? Neglect leap years. Solution of this and similar problems is facilitated by use of a log table and an adding machine.

6. Two cards are drawn at random from a 52-card deck. What is the probability that they are the queen of spades and the jack of diamonds?

7. A drawer contains 10 white socks, 10 red ones, and 10 black ones. If their owner arises early and picks out socks in the dark, what is the probability of getting a pair if he picks out two? Three? Four?

8. A carpenter has a tool chest with two compartments, each one having a lock. He has two keys for each lock, and he keeps all four keys on the same ring. His habitual procedure in opening a compartment is to select a key at random and try it. If it fails, he selects one of the remaining three and tries it, and so on. What is the probability that he succeeds on the first try? The second? The third? Would he gain efficiency if he removed one key for each lock, leaving only one of each kind? Explain.

9. In a table of two-digit random numbers, what is the probability that the digit 3 appears exactly once in a two-digit number? Try to make the calculation without listing all the two-digit numbers.

10. A series of observations of the focal length of a lens was made by focusing an image of a distant object (such as the moon) on a screen. The measurements, made to the nearest $\frac{1}{10}$ mm, grouped themselves around the true value with the following probabilities:

Error, mm	Probability
0.3	0.04
0.2	0.10
0.1	0.20
0.0	0.25
−0.1	0.20
−0.2	0.10
−0.3	0.04

a. What is the probability that a single measurement will be in error by more than ±0.15 mm?

b. If three measurements are made, what is the probability that their errors are 0.1, 0.0, and −0.1 mm, respectively?

c. What is the probability that the errors in part b will occur, *in any order?*

11. In a batch of 1000 light bulbs, 10% were defective. If a sample of 10 bulbs is taken at random, what is the probability that none of the sample is defective? One? More than one?

12. In Prob. 11, suppose that the percentage of defective bulbs is not known, but in two samples of 10 bulbs each, two were found to be defective in each sample. What conclusions about the total number of defective bulbs ·can be made?

13. One die is rolled until 1 appears. What is the prob-

ability that this will happen on the first roll? The second? The third? The nth? Verify that the sum of these probabilities is unity. (*Hint:* Use the formula for the sum of an infinite geometric progression, $1 + a + a^2 + a^3 + \cdots = 1/(1 - a)$, for $a < 1$.)

14. How many different basketball teams (5 men) can be chosen from a group of 10 men, if each man can play any position?

15. The Explorers' Club has 30 members; an Executive Committee of four is to be chosen. How many possible committees are there?

16. If the Carnegie Tech tennis team has 10 men and the University of Pittsburgh team 7 men, how many different doubles matches between Tech and Pitt can be arranged?

17. How many distinct five-letter words can be formed with the English alphabet, if each word must contain two vowels and three consonants? (There are 5 vowels and 21 consonants in the alphabet.)

18. Four cards are drawn at random from a 52-card deck. What is the probability that they are the four aces?

19. In bridge, what is the probability that a certain player will be dealt a hand containing all 13 spades? (Write an expression, but do not carry out the long arithmetic computations.) Is the probability that *someone* at the table will receive this hand the same or different? Explain.

20. In poker, what is the probability of being dealt four of a kind (e.g., four aces, etc.) in a five-card hand? Does this depend on the number of players in the game?

21. Show that if a needle of length a is dropped at random on an array of parallel lines spaced $2a$ apart, the needle lands on a line with probability $1/\pi$.

Probability

22. A machine cuts out paper rectangles at random. Each dimension is between 1 and 2 in., but all values between these limits are equally likely. What is the probability that the area of a rectangle is greater than 2 in.^{2}?

CHAPTER III

PROBABILITY DISTRIBUTIONS

We have seen in Sec. 4 how some simple probabilities can be computed from elementary considerations. For more detailed analysis of probability we need to consider more efficient ways of dealing with probabilities of whole classes of events. For this purpose we introduce the concept of a *probability distribution*.

6 | The Meaning of a Probability Distribution

To introduce the idea of a probability distribution, suppose that we flip 10 pennies at the same time. We can compute in an elementary way the probability that four will come down heads and the other six tails. But suppose we ask: What is the probability for the appearance of five heads and five tails, or seven heads and three tails, or more generally, for n heads and $(10 - n)$ tails, where n may be any integer between 0 and 10? The answer to this question is a set of numbers, one for each value of n. These numbers can be thought of as forming a *function* of n, $f(n)$. That is, for each n there is a value of $f(n)$ which gives the probability of the event characterized by the number n. Such a function is called a *probability distribution*.

A probability distribution is always defined for a definite range of values of the index n. In the above example, n is an integer between 0 and 10. If, as will usually be the case in our problems, this range of the index includes all the possible events, then the sum of all the probabilities must be unity (certainty). In this case,

$$\sum_n f(n) = 1 \tag{6.1}$$

where the sum extends over the entire range of values of n appropriate to the particular problem under consideration.

An example of a probability distribution which can be obtained using the methods of Sec. 4 is the probability of various results from rolling two dice. The total may be any integer from 2 to 12, but these numbers are not all equally likely. We saw in Sec. 4, in fact, that the probability for 7 was $\frac{1}{6}$, while the probability for 11 was $\frac{1}{18}$. Expressing these facts in the language just introduced, we let n be the total on the two dice, and $f(n)$ be the probability for this number. We have found that $f(7) = \frac{1}{6}$ and $f(11) = \frac{1}{18}$. The other values for this distribution can be obtained similarly; the whole distribution is as follows:

n	$f(n)$
2	$\frac{1}{36}$
3	$\frac{1}{18}$
4	$\frac{1}{12}$
5	$\frac{1}{9}$
6	$\frac{5}{36}$
7	$\frac{1}{6}$
8	$\frac{5}{36}$
9	$\frac{1}{9}$
10	$\frac{1}{12}$
11	$\frac{1}{18}$
12	$\frac{1}{36}$

According to Eq. (6.1), the sum of all the values of $f(n)$ should be unity. The reader is invited to verify that this is in fact the case. The distribution $f(n)$ can be represented graphically by means of a histogram, as shown in Fig. 6.1.

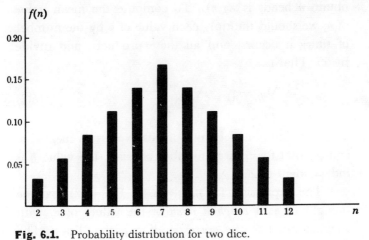

Fig. 6.1. Probability distribution for two dice.

Of course, the probability distribution may have more than one index. If we flip 10 pennies and 4 dimes, we can compute the probability that among the pennies there will be n heads, and that among the dimes there will be r, where n is an integer between 0 and 10, and r is an integer between 0 and 4. We can call the result $f(n,r)$ to indicate that the probability depends on both n and r. We shall not discuss such probability distributions in this text; they are treated by straightforward extensions of the methods to be discussed here.

Returning to the 10-penny problem, suppose that we want to find the *average* or *mean* number of heads in a large number of trials. Suppose we flip the pennies Z times, where Z is a very large number. By definition of the probability distribution, the number of times we obtain n heads is $Zf(n)$. To compute the mean value of n, we should multiply each value of n by the number of times it occurs, add all these products, and divide by Z. That is,

$$\bar{n} = \frac{1}{Z} \sum_n nZf(n) = \sum_n nf(n) \tag{6.2}$$

The fact that Z cancels out of this expression means, of course, that for a large number of trials, the value $\bar{n}$ is independent of Z.

The expression for $\bar{n}$, given by Eq. (6.2), can be thought of as a *weighted mean* of the values of n, with weights equal to the corresponding probabilities. The sum of the weights in this case is unity.

As an illustration of the meaning of Eq. (6.2), we use the distribution for two dice to compute the *mean* value of the total, in a large number of rolls. We multiply each value of n by its probability and add the results:

n	$f(n)$	$nf(n)$
2	$\frac{1}{36}$	$\frac{1}{18}$
3	$\frac{1}{18}$	$\frac{3}{18}$
4	$\frac{1}{12}$	$\frac{1}{3}$ or $\frac{6}{18}$
5	$\frac{1}{9}$	$\frac{5}{9}$ or $\frac{10}{18}$
6	$\frac{5}{36}$	$\frac{5}{6}$ or $\frac{15}{18}$
7	$\frac{1}{6}$	$\frac{7}{6}$ or $\frac{21}{18}$
8	$\frac{5}{36}$	$\frac{10}{9}$ or $\frac{20}{18}$
9	$\frac{1}{9}$	1 or $\frac{18}{18}$
10	$\frac{1}{12}$	$\frac{5}{6}$ or $\frac{15}{18}$
11	$\frac{1}{18}$	$\frac{11}{18}$
12	$\frac{1}{36}$	$\frac{1}{3}$ or $\frac{6}{18}$
	$\bar{n} = \Sigma \, nf(n) = \frac{126}{18} = 7$	

The average value of n is $\bar{n} = 7$. This should not be surprising; the probabilities are distributed symmetrically about $n = 7$ so that, roughly speaking, a value of n greater than 7 is as probable as a value smaller than 7 by the same amount.

In the same manner one could calculate the mean value of n^2, which is

$$\bar{n}^2 = \sum_n n^2 f(n) \tag{6.3}$$

More commonly, one is interested in the average value of $(n - \bar{n})^2$, which is of course the *variance* of the values of n which occur. This is given in general by

$$\sigma^2 = \sum_n (n - \bar{n})^2 f(n) \tag{6.4}$$

As an example of the use of Eq. (6.4), we compute the variance of the two-dice distribution. The calculation is conveniently arranged in tabular form as follows:

n	$(n - \bar{n})$	$(n - \bar{n})^2$	$f(n)$	$(n - \bar{n})^2 f(n)$
2	-5	25	$\frac{1}{36}$	$\frac{25}{36}$
3	-4	16	$\frac{1}{18}$	$\frac{32}{36}$
4	-3	9	$\frac{1}{12}$	$\frac{27}{36}$
5	-2	4	$\frac{1}{9}$	$\frac{16}{36}$
6	-1	1	$\frac{5}{36}$	$\frac{5}{36}$
7	0	0	$\frac{1}{6}$	0
8	1	1	$\frac{5}{36}$	$\frac{5}{36}$
9	2	4	$\frac{1}{9}$	$\frac{16}{36}$
10	3	9	$\frac{1}{12}$	$\frac{27}{36}$
11	4	16	$\frac{1}{18}$	$\frac{32}{36}$
12	5	25	$\frac{1}{36}$	$\frac{25}{36}$

$$\sigma^2 = \Sigma \, (n - \bar{n})^2 f(n) = \frac{105}{36} = 2\frac{11}{12}$$

Thus the root-mean-square spread of the values of n about the mean is $\sigma = \left(\frac{35}{12}\right)^{1/2} = 1.71$, which is about what we would guess from looking at the distribution.

So far we have discussed probability distributions based on the definition of probability given in Sec. 4, which in turn is based on the idea of making an indefinitely large number of trials, counting the number of favorable events, and taking the ratio of the two. Our discussion of the mean and standard deviation is based on the assumption that a very large number of trials has been made.

It may not be immediately clear, therefore, how these quantities are related to the results which would be obtained if we made an experiment consisting of a relatively small number of trials. If there is only one trial, for example, the mean is clearly not very likely to equal the mean for an infinite number of trials. The mean $\bar{n}$ for a small number of trials cannot be expected to correspond exactly with the value obtained with an infinite number of trials. The same is true for the standard deviation of a small number of trials.

To describe the distinction between the infinitely large number of trials used to define $f(n)$ and any small number of trials in an actual experiment, we call $f(n)$ the *infinite parent distribution* and the results of any group of trials a *sample* of this distribution. It is clear that the mean of a small sample is only an *estimate* of the mean of the infinite parent distribution. For *some* types of distributions it can be shown that the precision of this estimate increases with the size of the sample, but it is important to remember that it is never more than an estimate. Similarly, the standard deviation of a sample is an estimate of the standard deviation of the infinite parent distribution.

Moreover, there are good theoretical reasons, which

we shall not discuss in detail, for stating that Eq. (3.9) does not even give the *best* estimate of the parent distribution standard deviation which can be obtained from a given sample. It turns out that a somewhat better estimate is given by

$$\sigma = \sqrt{\frac{1}{N-1} \sum_{i=1}^{N} (x_i - \bar{x})^2} \qquad (6.5)$$

which differs from Eq. (3.9) in that the sum of the d_i^2 is divided by $(N-1)$ instead of N. Roughly speaking, the reason for this is that the deviations are not all independent; the same data have been used previously to compute the sample mean which is used to compute the d_i^2, and so the number of *independent* deviations is only $(N-1)$. Although this modification is of some theoretical significance, it is not usually of any *practical* importance. Ordinarily N is sufficiently large so that the sample standard deviation is affected very little by the choice between N and $(N-1)$.

Because we shall sometimes want to learn as precisely as possible the characteristics of the infinite parent distribution, it is important to know how well the mean and standard deviation of the sample approximate the mean and the standard deviation of the infinite parent distribution, and how the precision of these approximations depends on the size of the sample. We return to these questions in Chap. IV.

A related question arises if we have a number of trials of some kind and want to ascertain whether the results of these trials can or cannot be regarded as a sample of some particular infinite parent distribution. The distribution of results of a small sample, as we have just pointed out, will not be identical to that of the infinite parent distribution in any case; but how close should we expect the sample distribution to be to the

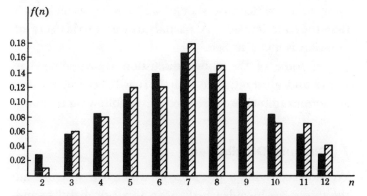

Fig. 6.2. Comparison of parent and sample distributions for two dice. The solid bars represent the parent distribution, the shaded bars the distribution which resulted from a sample of 100 rolls. The mean of the parent distribution is exactly 7, while the mean of the sample is 7.15.

infinite parent distribution in order to conclude that the sample is in fact a sample of this parent distribution? A partial answer to this question is given in Sec. 11.

A very practical example of this kind of question arises in connection with the probability distribution for two dice, shown in Fig. 6.1. Suppose we want to determine whether the dice of a particular pair are loaded. If they are loaded, their parent distrib ion will not be that of Fig. 6.1, but something different. We roll the dice several times, recording the results. We then need a means of comparing this sample distribution with the parent distribution characteristic of unloaded dice. How much difference between the sample and parent distributions should be expected if the dice are *not* loaded? How much difference should we require as evidence that they *are* loaded? A partial answer to this sort of question is given in Sec. 11.

If some of the above discussion seems somewhat vague and abstract, take heart! It will become clearer as more examples are discussed in the following sections.

7 | Binomial Distribution

We now consider a problem in which we will use all the things we have learned so far about probability and statistics. Suppose that we have N independent events of some kind, each of which has probability p of succeeding and probability $(1 - p)$ of not succeeding. We want to know the probability that exactly n of the events will succeed.

An example may help clarify the situation. Suppose we light five firecrackers. They are supposedly identical, but because of some uncertainty in their manufacture only ¾ of them explode when lighted. In other words, the probability for any one to explode is $p = ¾$, and the probability that it will fizzle is $1 - p = ¼$. In this case the number of independent events, N, is 5.

We now ask for the probability that, of these 5, n will explode when lighted, where n is an integer between 0 and 5.

A few particular cases are easy. If the probability of success in one of these events is p, the probability that all N of them will succeed is p^N. The probability that all N will fail is $(1 - p)^N$. In our example, the probability that all five firecrackers will explode is $(\frac{3}{4})^5 = 0.237$. The probability that none will explode is $(\frac{1}{4})^5 = 0.00098$. In other words, neither of these is very likely; probability favors the other possibilities in which *some* of the firecrackers explode. The various probabilities are shown graphically in Fig. 7.1.

The in-between possibilities are not so simple. If we select a particular group of n events from N, the probability that these n will succeed and all the rest $(N - n)$ will fail is $p^n(1 - p)^{N-n}$. We can shorten the notations slightly by abbreviating $1 - p = q$.

This is not yet the probability that exactly n events will succeed, because we have considered only one particular group or combination of n events. How many combinations of n events can be chosen from N? Just the number of combinations of N things taken n at a time. So the probability that exactly n events will succeed from the group of N, which we denote by $f_{N,p}(n)$, is

$$f_{N,p}(n) = \binom{N}{n} p^n q^{N-n} \tag{7.1}$$

which we can call the probability of n successes in N

trials if the probability of success in one trial is p. This expression $f_{N,p}(n)$, defined by Eq. (7.1), is called the *binomial distribution* because of its close relation to the

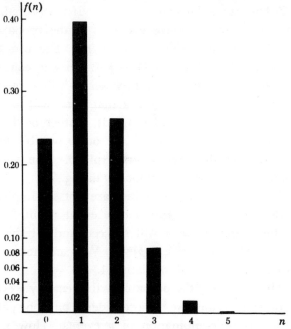

Fig. 7.1. Probability that n firecrackers will not explode in a group of five, if the probability for any one to explode is $\frac{3}{4}$. This is a binomial distribution with $N = 5$, $p = \frac{3}{4}$.

binomial theorem. A few examples of binomial distributions, computed from Eq. (7.1), are shown in Fig. 7.2.

What is the binomial distribution good for? Here is another example. Suppose we roll three dice. We know that the probability for 5 to come up on a single die is ⅙. What is the probability of 5 coming up on n dice, where n can be 0, 1, 2, or 3? We see that this is

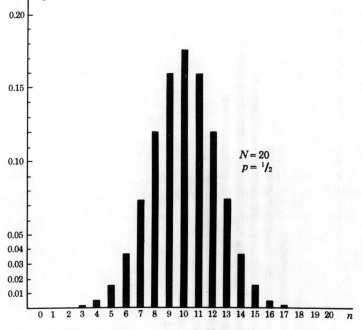

Fig. 7.2a. Example of binomial distribution, with $N = 20$. Distribution for $p = ½$ is symmetric about the mean, $\bar{n} = 10$.

exactly the problem solved by the binomial distribution. The probability of success in a single trial is ⅙ in this case, so that $p = ⅙$. We are asking for the probability of n successes in three trials. This is, according to the binomial distribution,

Probability Distributions

$$f_{3,1/6}(n) = \binom{3}{n}\left(\frac{1}{6}\right)^n\left(1 - \frac{1}{6}\right)^{3-n}$$

The probabilities of 0, 1, 2, and successes in three trials are then

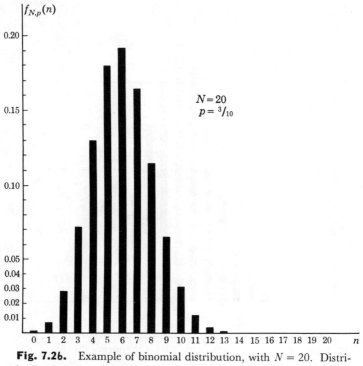

$$N = 20$$
$$p = {}^3/_{10}$$

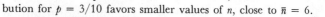

Fig. 7.26. Example of binomial distribution, with $N = 20$. Distribution for $p = 3/10$ favors smaller values of n, close to $\bar{n} = 6$.

Zero successes: $f_{3,1/6}(0) = \dfrac{3!}{(3-0)!\,0!}\left(\dfrac{5}{6}\right)^3 \quad = \dfrac{125}{216}$

One success: $f_{3,1/6}(1) = \dfrac{3!}{(3-1)!\,1!}\left(\dfrac{1}{6}\right)\left(\dfrac{5}{6}\right)^2 = \dfrac{75}{216}$

Two successes: $\quad f_{3,1/6}(2) = \dfrac{3!}{(3-2)!\,2!}\left(\dfrac{1}{6}\right)^{2}\left(\dfrac{5}{6}\right) = \dfrac{15}{216}$

Three successes: $f_{3,1/6}(3) = \dfrac{3!}{(3-3)!\,3!}\left(\dfrac{1}{6}\right)^{3} \quad\;\; = \dfrac{1}{216}$

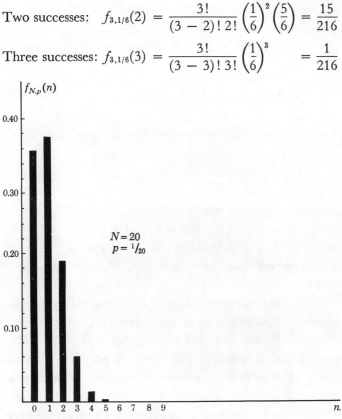

Fig. 7.2c. Example of binomial distribution, with $N = 20$. Distribution is strongly asymmetric. Here $\bar{n} = 1$, and probabilities for $n > 6$ are negligibly small.

As a check on these calculations we note that the total probability for 0, 1, 2, or 3 successes must be one since there are no other possibilities. Thus, the four probabilities which we have calculated above must total unity; this is in fact the case.

More generally, it must be true, for the same reason, that

$$\sum_{n=0}^{N} f_{N,p}(n) = \sum_{n=0}^{N} \binom{N}{n} p^n q^{N-n} = 1 \tag{7.2}$$

To show that this is in fact the case, we note that

$$\sum_{n=0}^{N} \binom{N}{n} p^n q^{N-n} \tag{7.3}$$

is exactly equal to the binomial expansion of $(q + p)^N$, as seen from Eq. (5.6). But $p + q = 1$, so $(q + p)^N = 1$, and Eq. (7.2) is established. Note, incidentally, that it is true for *any* value of p, which is a number between 0 and 1.

Now that we have calculated the probability for any number of successes in N trials, we can calculate the *mean* (or average) number of successes in N trials. The meaning of this mean is the same as in Sec. 6. We make the N trials, observing a certain number n of successes. We make N trials *again*, finding in general a different number of successes. We do this a large number of times, say Z (where Z may stand for a zillion), and then compute the *mean* of all the numbers of successes which we observe.

To do this, we multiply each number of successes n by the number of times $Z f_{N,p}(n)$ that it occurs, and then divide by the total number of sets of trials, Z. The average number of successes, which we denote by $\bar{n}$, is

$$\bar{n} = \sum_{n=0}^{N} n \binom{N}{n} p^n (1 - p)^{N-n} \tag{7.4}$$

The sum ranges from $n = 0$ to N because in every one of the sets of trials *some* number of successes between 0 and N must occur. To summarize, we have obtained Eq. (7.4) directly from Eq. (6.2) by inserting the expression for the binomial distribution function, Eq. (7.1).

We can calculate the value of $\bar{n}$ if we know the number of trials N and the probability p for success in any one trial. In the example of three dice, we have used the values of N and p given ($N = 3, p = \frac{1}{6}$) to compute the values of the probability distribution $f_{3,1/6}(n)$. Using these values, we proceed as follows:

n	$f_{3,1/6}(n)$	$nf_{3,1/6}(n)$
0	$\frac{125}{216}$	0
1	$\frac{75}{216}$	$\frac{75}{216}$
2	$\frac{15}{216}$	$\frac{30}{216}$
3	$\frac{1}{216}$	$\frac{3}{216}$

$$\bar{n} = \sum_{n=0}^{3} f_{3,1/6}(n) = \frac{108}{216} = \frac{1}{2}$$

If we average the numbers of 5s in all the trials, the result is $\frac{1}{2}$. This is not equal to the result of any single trial, of course, and there is no reason to expect it to be. The most probable number is zero, and the probabilities for the others are just such as to make the average $\frac{1}{2}$.

This calculation can be done more simply, but to do it more simply we have to derive an equation which expresses the *result* of performing the sum in Eq. (7.4) in a simple way. Deriving the equation requires some acrobatics, the details of which are given in Appendix B. The result is

$$\bar{n} = \sum_{n=0}^{N} n \binom{N}{n} p^n (1 - p)^{N-n} = Np \tag{7.5}$$

This remarkably simple and very reasonable result says that the average number of successes in N trials is just the probability of success in any one trial, multiplied by the number of trials. If we had had to guess at a result, this is probably what we would have guessed!

Applying this result to the three-dice problem, we see that with $N = 3$ and $p = \frac{1}{6}$, the average number of 5s can be obtained immediately: $\bar{n} = Np = 3 \times \frac{1}{6} = \frac{1}{2}$, in agreement with our previous result.

Just as the mean $\bar{n}$ is defined in general for any distribution $f(n)$, by Eq. (6.2) the variance is obtained by calculating the mean of the squares of the deviations, Eq. (6.4). For the binomial distribution, the variance is given by

$$\sigma^2 = \sum_{n=0}^{N} (n - \bar{n})^2 f_{N,p}(n) = \sum_{n=0}^{N} (n - Np)^2 f_{N,p}(n), \tag{7.6}$$

in which we have used $\bar{n} = Np$, Eq. (7.5).

Evaluation of this sum, as with the evaluation of $\bar{n}$, requires a bit of trickery. The details are again given in Appendix B so as not to interrupt the continuity of the present discussion. The result of the calculation is

$$\sigma^2 = Np(1 - p) = Npq \tag{7.7}$$

or

$$\sigma = \sqrt{Npq} \tag{7.8}$$

another remarkably simple result.

As an illustration of the properties of the binomial distribution just obtained, we return to the example of three dice, for which we have computed the probabilities for the occurrence of any number of 5s between 0 and 3. In this case, $N = 3$, $p = \frac{1}{6}$. The mean number of 5s was found to be $\frac{1}{2}$. Similarly, we may compute the standard deviation:

$$\sigma = \sqrt{Npq} = \sqrt{3 \times \frac{1}{6} \times \frac{5}{6}} = 0.646$$

which means that the root-mean-square deviation of the values of n about the mean ($\bar{n} = \frac{1}{2}$) is somewhat less than unity. The deviations of the few events for which $n = 2$ or $n = 3$ are, of course, larger than this.

8 | Poisson Distribution

We consider next a particular application of the binomial distribution which is important in nuclear physics. Suppose that we have N radioactive nuclei. Suppose also that the probability for any one of these to undergo a radioactive decay in a given interval of time (T, for instance) is p. We want to know the probability that

n nuclei will decay in the interval T. The answer is of course the old familiar binomial distribution function $f_{N,p}(n)$. This is, however, somewhat unwieldy for practical calculations; N may be a very large number, such as 10^{23}, and p may be the order of 10^{-20} or so. With numbers of these magnitudes, there is no practical way to evaluate the binomial distribution, Eq. (7.1).

Fortunately, we can make considerable simplifications by using approximations which are valid when N is extremely large and p is extremely small. We therefore consider the *limit* of the binomial distribution function as N grows very large and p grows very small in such a way that the *mean* of the distribution, which is Np, remains finite. We denote this product by

$$Np = a \tag{8.1}$$

We shall introduce the approximations in a manner which will make them seem plausible, but no attempt will be made to attain mathematical rigor.

First of all, we note that if p is a very small quantity, the average number of events will be very much smaller than N so that the values of n which are of interest will be extremely small compared to N. Guided by this observation, we make two approximations in the expression

$$f_{N,p}(n) = \frac{N!}{(N-n)!\,n!}\,p^n(1-p)^{N-n}$$

Consider first the factor

$$\frac{N!}{(N - n)!} = N(N - 1)(N - 2) \cdots (N - n + 1)$$

$$(8.2)$$

This is a product of n factors, none of which is significantly different from N. We therefore replace Eq. (8.2) by N^n. We then have approximately

$$f_{N,p}(n) \cong \frac{(Np)^n}{n!} (1 - p)^{N-n} = \frac{(Np)^n}{n!} \frac{(1 - p)^N}{(1 - p)^n}$$

$$(8.3)$$

Second, we notice that the factor $(1 - p)^n$ is very nearly equal to unity because it is a number very close to unity raised to a not terribly large power. We therefore drop this factor. We also eliminate N from the expression, using $a = Np$, and rearrange it to obtain

$$f(n) = \frac{a^n}{n!} (1 - p)^{a/p} = \frac{a^n}{n!} [(1 - p)^{1/p}]^a \qquad (8.4)$$

All that remains now is to evaluate the limit

$$\lim_{p \to 0} (1 - p)^{1/p}$$

This limit is discussed in many books on elementary calculus and is shown to have the value $1/e$. Using this fact in Eq. (8.4), we obtain

$$f_a(n) = \frac{a^n e^{-a}}{n!} \qquad (8.5)$$

This form is known as the Poisson distribution function. Note that while the binomial distribution contained two independent parameters (N and p), the Poisson distribution has only one (a). The other one disappeared when we took the limit of the binomial distribution as $N \to \infty$.

Using the definition of a, Eq. (8.1), and the general expression for the mean of the binomial distribution, Eq. (7.5), we find that the mean value of n is

$$\bar{n} = a \tag{8.6}$$

That is, if we observe the radioactive material for a series of time intervals T, recording the number of disintegrations taking place in each interval, we find that the *average* number of disintegrations is a.

As with the general form of the binomial distribution, if we add the probabilities for all possible values of n, we must obtain unity (certainty). That is,

$$\sum_{n=0}^{\infty} f_a(n) = 1 \tag{8.7}$$

We extend the summation from zero to infinity because we have let the number of independent events N become indefinitely large. To establish that Eq. (8.7) is in fact true, we insert Eq. (8.5) in Eq. (8.7):

$$\sum_{n=0}^{\infty} f_a(n) = e^{-a} \sum_{n=0}^{\infty} \frac{a^n}{n!} \tag{8.8}$$

But the sum in Eq. (8.8) is nothing but the Maclaurin series expansion of the quantity e^a. Thus the sum in Eq. (8.7) does equal unity, as required.

Any probability distribution which is constructed so that the *sum* of the probabilities of all possible events is unity is said to be *normalized*. It is quite possible to define a probability distribution differently so that the sum of all the probabilities is a number different from unity. In this case, certainty is represented not by unity, but by some other number. It is usually convenient, however, to construct the probability distribution in such a way that the sum of all the probabilities is unity. This practice is followed everywhere in this book.

As has been stated in Eq. (8.6), the mean value of n for the Poisson distribution is simply $\bar{n} = a$. The standard deviation for the Poisson distribution can also be obtained easily from the expression for the standard deviation of the binomial distribution, Eq. (7.8), by using $Np = a$ and the fact that q is very nearly unity; the result is simply

$$\sigma = \sqrt{a} \qquad \text{or} \qquad \sigma^2 = a \qquad (8.9)$$

Here is an example of the use of the Poisson distribution in radioactive decay. Suppose we have 10^{20} atoms of Shakespeareum, a fictitious radioactive element whose nuclei emit α particles. Shakespeareum might be, for example, a rare unstable isotope of one of the rare-earth elements, with an atomic weight in the vicinity of 150; in this case 10^{20} atoms correspond to about 25 mg of the element. Suppose that the decay constant is 2×10^{-20} per second, which means that the probability for any one nucleus to decay in 1 sec is 2×10^{-20}. This corresponds to a half-life of about 10^{12} years, rather long but not impossibly so.

Now suppose we observe this sample of material for many 1-sec intervals. What is the probability to observe *no* α emissions in an interval? One? Two? The answers are given simply by the Poisson distribution. We are given $N = 10^{20}$ and $p = 2 \times 10^{-20}$; so we have $a = 2$. Substituting this value in Eq. (8.5), we obtain the following values:

n	$f_2(n)$
0	0.135
1	0.271
2	0.271
3	0.180
4	0.090
5	0.036
6	0.012
7	0.003
8	0.001

These results are shown graphically in Fig. 8.1. The mean number of counts in this case is exactly 2, and the standard deviation is $\sqrt{2}$. For comparison, Fig. 8.2 shows a Poisson distribution with $a = 10$.

In many practical applications of the Poisson distribution the problem may be somewhat different, in that the constant a may not be known at the beginning. The problem may be, for example, to determine the value of a from a distribution of experimental data. If it is known that the parent distribution of which the data are a sample is a Poisson distribution, then the best estimate of a is just the mean of the sample distribu-

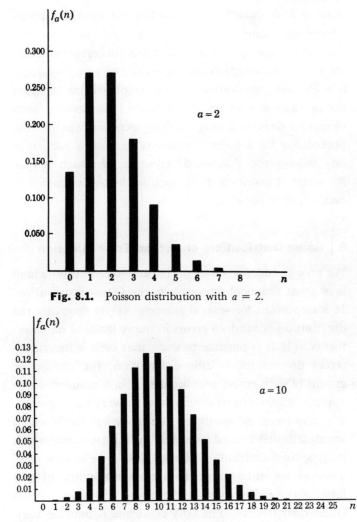

Fig. 8.1. Poisson distribution with $a = 2$.

Fig. 8.2. Poisson distribution with $a = 10$.

tion. A little thought will show that the standard deviation of this value is $\sqrt{a}$.

Other cases may arise where it is not certain whether the parent distribution corresponding to a given sample *is* a Poisson distribution. For example, if one observes the number of eggs laid by a flock of chickens on each of several days, one may want to ascertain whether the probability for a given number of eggs on a particular day follows the Poisson distribution. In such a case some test of goodness of fit, such as the test discussed in Sec. 11, may be used.

9 | Gauss Distribution, or Normal Error Function

We now consider another probability distribution which is of great practical importance, the Gauss distribution. It is important for several reasons. (1) It describes the distribution of random errors in many kinds of measurements. (2) It is possible to show that even if individual errors do not follow this distribution, the *averages* of groups of such errors are distributed in a manner which approaches the Gauss distribution for very large groups. We may have, for example, a set of observations which are distributed according to the *xyz* distribution, which may be any distribution at all. If we take groups of N observations and average them, then in the limit of very large N the *averages* will be distributed according to the Gauss distribution. The only condition is that the variance of the *xyz* distribution be finite. This statement is known as the central-limit theorem; it is very important in more advanced developments in mathematical statistics.

The Gauss distribution can be regarded in two ways: as a result which can be derived mathematically from elementary considerations or as a formula found empirically to agree with random errors which actually occur in a given measurement. Someone has remarked, in fact, that everyone believes that the Gauss distribution describes the distribution of random errors, mathematicians because they think physicists have verified it experimentally, and physicists because they think mathematicians have proved it theoretically!

From a theoretical point of view, we can make the plausible assumption that any random error can be thought of as the result of a large number of elementary errors, all of equal magnitude, and each equally likely to be positive or negative. The Gauss distribution can therefore be associated with a limiting form of the binomial distribution in which the number of independent events N (corresponding to the elementary errors) becomes very large, while the probability p of success in each (the chance of any elementary error being positive) is ½. The derivation of the Gauss distribution from these considerations is given in Appendix C.

Many people feel, however, that the real justification for using the Gauss distribution to describe distribution of random errors is that many sets of experimental observations turn out to obey it. This is a more convincing reason than any mathematical derivation. Hence it is a valid point of view to treat this distribution as an experimental fact, state its formula dogmatically, and then examine what it means and what it is good for.

The Gauss distribution function is often referred to as the *normal error function*, and errors distributed according to the Gauss distribution are said to be *normally distributed*.

The Gauss distribution is

$$f(x) = Ae^{-h^2(x-m)^2} \tag{9.1}$$

where A, h, and m are constants and x is the value obtained from one measurement. This distribution differs from those we have considered previously in that we shall regard x as a continuous variable, rather than an integer as with the binomial and Poisson distributions. This will necessitate some further discussion of the significance of $f(x)$; but first we plot the function $f(x)$ to get a general idea of its behavior.

Figure 9.1 is a graph of the Gauss distribution function, Eq. (9.1). We note that A is the maximum height of the function, m represents the value of x for which the function attains this maximum height, and h has something to do with the broadness or narrowness of the bell-shaped curve. A large value of h corresponds to a narrow, peaked curve, while a small value of h gives a broad, flat curve.

Now, what is the significance of the function $f(x)$? We are tempted to say that $f(x)$ represents the probability of observing the value x of the measured quantity. But this is not really correct. Remembering that x is a continuous variable, we realize that the probability for x to have *exactly* any particular value is zero. What we must discuss instead is the probability that x will have a value in a certain region, say between x and $x + \Delta x$.

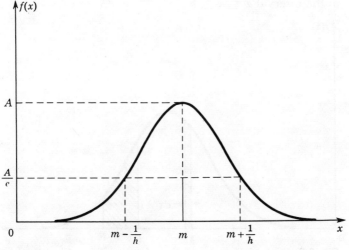

Fig. 9.1. Gauss distribution function. The points $x = m \pm 1/h$, at which the curve has $1/e$ of its maximum height, are shown.

So the proper interpretation of the function $f(x)$ is that for a small interval dx, $f(x)\,dx$ represents the probability of observing a measurement which lies in the interval between x and $x + dx$.

This statement has a simple graphical interpretation. In Fig. 9.2, the area of the shaded strip on the graph represents $f(x)\,dx$. Therefore we can say that the *area* under the curve within the interval dx represents the probability that a measurement will fall in this interval. Similarly,

$$P(a,b) = \int_a^b f(x)\, dx \qquad (9.2)$$

is the probability that a measurement will fall somewhere in the interval $a \leq x \leq b$.

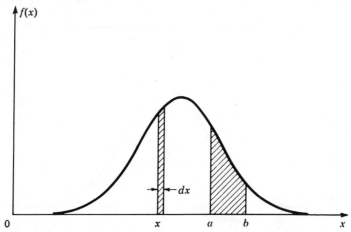

Fig. 9.2. Graphical representation of probabilities. Shaded areas represent probabilities for an observation to fall in the corresponding intervals.

The total probability for a measurement to fall *somewhere* is of course unity; so the total area under curve $f(x)$ must be unity. Analytically, we can say that it must be true that

$$\int_{-\infty}^{\infty} f(x)\, dx = 1 \qquad (9.3)$$

This is analogous to Eq. (6.1). If this condition is satisfied, the function $f(x)$ is said to be normalized in the same sense as the functions in Secs. 7 and 8 were normalized, having a total probability of 1. We have extended the range of integration from $-\infty$ to $+\infty$ because it is necessary to include all possible values of x in the integration.

The requirement that the function $f(x)$ be normalized imposes a restriction on the constants which appear in the function. If we know h and m, then

$$\int_{-\infty}^{\infty} Ae^{-h^2(x-m)^2} \, dx = 1 \qquad (9.4)$$

will be satisfied only with one particular value of the constant A. To obtain this value of A, we must actually perform the integration. To simplify the integral we make a change of variable, letting

$$h(x - m) = z \qquad (9.5)$$

Equation (9.4) then becomes

$$A \int_{-\infty}^{\infty} e^{-z^2} \, dz = h \qquad (9.6)$$

The value of the integral in Eq. (9.6) can be shown to be

$$\int_{-\infty}^{\infty} e^{-z^2} \, dz = \sqrt{\pi} \qquad (9.7)$$

Obtaining this value requires a small chicanery, the details of which are given in Appendix D. Inserting Eq. (9.7) in Eq. (9.6),

$$A = \frac{h}{\sqrt{\pi}} \qquad (9.8)$$

Thus, we find that in order to satisfy the normalization condition, Eq. (9.4), the constant A must have the value $A = h/\sqrt{\pi}$. From now on, therefore, we write the Gauss distribution function as

$$f(x) = \frac{h}{\sqrt{\pi}} e^{-h^2(x-m)^2} \qquad (9.9)$$

which is normalized for every value of h.

Next, we find the mean value of x for this distribution. The meaning of *mean* is the same as always—the average of a very large number of measurements of the quantity x. We could go through the same line of reasoning as in Sec. 6 by introducing the total number of measurements Z and then showing that it divides out of the final result. Instead, we observe simply that $f(x)\, dx$ represents the probability of occurrence of the measurement in the interval dx and that the mean value of x is found simply by integrating the product of this probability and the value of x corresponding to this interval. That is,

$$\bar{x} = \int_{-\infty}^{\infty} xf(x)\, dx \qquad (9.10)$$

This expression is completely analogous to Eq. (6.2); we use an integral here rather than a sum because x is a continuous variable rather than a discrete one.

To compute $\bar{x}$ we insert Eq. (9.9) into Eq. (9.10) and make the change of variable given by Eq. (9.5):

$$\bar{x} = \frac{h}{\sqrt{\pi}} \int_{-\infty}^{\infty} xe^{-h^2(x-m)^2}\, dx$$

$$= \frac{1}{\sqrt{\pi}} \int \left(\frac{z}{h} + m \right) e^{-z^2}\, dz \qquad (9.11)$$

The first term of this expression integrates to zero because the contributions from negative values of z exactly cancel those from positive values. The part that survives is

$$\bar{x} = \frac{m}{\sqrt{\pi}} \int_{-\infty}^{\infty} e^{-z^2} \, dz = \frac{m}{\sqrt{\pi}} \sqrt{\pi}$$

$$= m \tag{9.12}$$

a result which we could have guessed in the first place simply by looking at the graph of the function.

The calculation of the variance proceeds in a similar manner. The variance is given by

$$\sigma^2 = \int_{-\infty}^{\infty} (x - m)^2 f(x) \, dx$$

$$= \int_{-\infty}^{\infty} \frac{h}{\sqrt{\pi}} (x - m)^2 e^{-h^2(x-m)^2} \, dx \tag{9.13}$$

To evaluate this integral we make the change of variable, Eq. (9.5), to obtain

$$\sigma^2 \doteq \frac{1}{h^2 \sqrt{\pi}} \int_{-\infty}^{\infty} z^2 e^{-z^2} \, dz \tag{9.14}$$

This is a convergent integral; at large values of z, z^2 becomes very large, but e^{-z^2} grows small so rapidly that the product $z^2 e^{-z^2}$ also approaches zero very rapidly. The integral in Eq. (9.14) can be integrated by parts to convert it into the form of Eq. (9.7), whose value is known. The final result is

$$\sigma^2 = \frac{1}{2h^2} \qquad \text{or} \qquad \sigma = \frac{1}{\sqrt{2}\, h} \tag{9.15}$$

The standard deviation is inversely proportional to h. This should not be surprising, because larger values of h mean a more sharply peaked curve as well as smaller values of σ. Since h is large for sharply peaked curves,

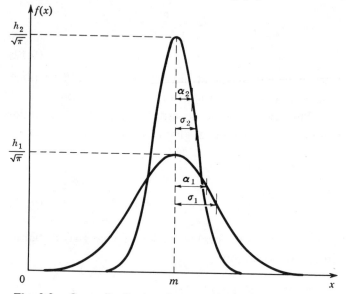

Fig. 9.3. Gauss distributions for two values of h with the same m; $h_2 = 2h_1$. Positions of σ and α for the two curves are shown.

corresponding to small spread of errors, h is sometimes called the *measure of precision* of the distribution. The Gauss distribution is plotted in Fig. 9.3 for two values of h.

It is often useful to write the Gauss distribution in terms of σ rather than h. Using σ, the function becomes

$$f(x) = \frac{1}{\sqrt{2\pi}\,\sigma}\, e^{-(x-m)^2/2\sigma^2} \tag{9.16}$$

The *mean deviation* for the Gauss distribution is even easier to obtain than the variance. It is given by

$$\alpha = \int_{-\infty}^{\infty} |x - m|\, \frac{h}{\sqrt{\pi}}\, e^{-h^2(x-m)^2}\, dx$$

$$= \frac{2h}{\sqrt{\pi}} \int_{0}^{\infty} y e^{-h^2 y^2}\, dy \tag{9.17}$$

This integral can easily be evaluated by making the substitution $z = h^2 y^2$. It should not be necessary to give the details of this substitution; the result is simply

$$\alpha = \frac{1}{\sqrt{\pi}\,h} \tag{9.18}$$

Comparing this with Eq. (9.15), we see that for the Gauss distribution the standard deviation and mean deviation are proportional, since both are inversely proportional to h. The standard deviation is the larger of the two; the relation is

$$\sigma = \sqrt{\frac{\pi}{2}}\, \alpha = 1.25\, \alpha \tag{9.19}$$

This equation is quite useful when one wants a rough estimate of the standard deviation of a set of observations whose errors are thought to be normally distributed. Instead of calculating σ from the data, one calculates α (which is generally easier since it is not necessary to square all the deviations) and then uses Eq. (9.19). It must be emphasized, though, that this relationship holds only for the Gauss distribution; it is not valid for other distributions.

The Gauss distribution may be used to find the probability that a measurement will fall within any specified limits. In particular, it is of interest to calculate the probability that a measurement will fall within σ of the mean value. This will give a more clear understanding of the significance of the standard deviation. The probability P that a measurement will fall between $m - \sigma$ and $m + \sigma$ is given by

$$P = \int_{m-\sigma}^{m+\sigma} \frac{1}{\sqrt{2\pi}\,\sigma} e^{-(x-m)^2/2\sigma^2}\,dx \qquad (9.20)$$

Making a change of variable $t = (x - m)/\sigma$, we find

$$P = \frac{1}{\sqrt{2\pi}} \int_{-1}^{+1} e^{-t^2/2}\,dt \qquad (9.21)$$

This integral cannot be evaluated except by making numerical approximations. Fortunately, such integrals are used sufficiently often so that extensive tables of their values have been calculated. A short table of values of the integral

$$\frac{1}{\sqrt{2\pi}} \int_0^T e^{-t^2/2}\,dt$$

for various values of T is given at the end of the book, Table II. Also included for convenience is a table of values of the function $(1/\sqrt{2\pi})e^{-t^2/2}$, Table I. References to more extensive tables are also given.

In general, the probability for a measurement to occur in an interval within $T\sigma$ of the mean is

$$P(T) = \frac{1}{\sqrt{2\pi}} \int_{-T}^{T} e^{-t^2/2} \, dt \qquad (9.22)$$

The values of this probability for a few values of T are as follows:

$P(1) = 0.683 \qquad 1 - P(1) = 0.317$
$P(2) = 0.954 \qquad 1 - P(2) = 0.046$
$P(3) = 0.997 \qquad 1 - P(3) = 0.003$

These figures show that the probability for a measurement to fall within one standard deviation of the mean is about 68%; the probability that it will fall within two standard deviations is about 95%, and the probability that it will be *farther* away from the mean than three standard deviations is only 0.3%.

Here is an example of the use of some of the ideas just discussed. A surveyor runs a line over level ground between two points about 1000 ft apart. He carefully stretches his 100-ft tape to the proper tension for each segment of the measurement and applies the proper temperature correction, to eliminate systematic errors from these sources. He repeats the measurement 10 times. Supposing that the remaining errors are associated with random errors in the individual measurements, and that the resulting errors are randomly distributed, we can make the following calculations:

Observation (x), ft	$|d_i|$, ft
1023.56	0.055
1023.47	0.035
1023.51	0.005
1023.49	0.015
1023.51	0.005
1023.48	0.025
1023.50	0.005
1023.53	0.025
1023.48	0.025
1023.52	0.015
$\bar{x} = $ 1023.505 ft	0.210 ft

$$a = 0.021 \text{ ft}$$
$$\sigma = 1.25a = 0.026 \text{ ft}$$

The probability for an individual measurement to fall within 0.026 ft of the mean is 0.683, so we expect about 68% of the measurements to lie between 1023.48 and 1023.53 ft. The probability for falling within *two* standard deviations of the mean (1023.45 and 1023.56 ft) is 0.95, and so on. A more important question is: What is the reliability of the *mean?* This question can be answered with the methods introduced in Sec. 12.

10 | Rejection of Data

The question we consider next is a controversial one. It concerns the problem of what to do if, among a set of observations, one or more have deviations so large as to seem unreasonable. If, for example, a set of measurements made with a micrometer caliper has a standard deviation of 0.001 in., but one measurement differs from the mean by 0.010 in., then we are tempted to regard this large deviation as a blunder or mistake rather than a random error. What shall we do with this observation?

Such an observation creates an awkward situation for the experimenter. If he retains the questionable observation, it can have quite a large effect on the mean. It will also, of course, have an even greater effect on the standard deviation. If on the other hand it is discarded, one runs the risk of throwing away information which might lead to discovery of some unexpected phenomenon in the experiment. Important discoveries have resulted from apparently anomalous data. In any event, it cannot be denied that throwing away an observation constitutes tampering with the data, better known as "fudging."

As has been mentioned, this is a controversial question, and one which has been hotly debated. There is no agreement among authorities as to a definite answer. We therefore present several different points of view, and let the reader take his choice.

At one extreme, there is the point of view that unless there is a definite reason for suspecting that a particular observation is not valid, there is *never* any justification for throwing away data on purely statistical grounds, and that to do so is dishonest. If one takes this point of view, there is nothing more to say, except to advocate taking enough additional data so that the results are not affected much by the questionable observations.

At the other extreme is the point of view that an observation should be rejected if its occurrence is so improbable that it would not reasonably be expected to occur in the given set of data. We reason as follows: Suppose we make N measurements of a quantity; suppose that one of these seems to have an unusually large deviation. We use the Gauss distribution function to calculate the probability that a deviation this large or larger will occur. If this probability is larger than $1/N$, we conclude that it is reasonable to obtain such a deviation. If, on the other hand, the probability of obtaining such a deviation is much smaller than $1/N$, this means that it is very unlikely that such a large deviation should occur even once in a set of N measurements. In this case, we might consider rejecting this measurement as being due probably to a mistake or some anomalous fluctuation of the experimental conditions. We should expect occasionally to obtain deviations whose probabilities of occurrence may be *somewhat* smaller than $1/N$, but not a great deal smaller. One rule of thumb for rejection of data which is sometimes used is to reject an observation if the probability of obtaining it is less than $1/2N$. This criterion is known as *Chauvenet's criterion*.

Here is an example. Suppose we make 10 observations. According to Chauvenet's criterion, an observation should be disregarded if its deviation from the mean is so large that the probability of occurrence of a deviation that large or larger is less than $\frac{1}{20}$. Referring to Eq. (9.22), we want to find the value of T such that $P(T) = 1 - \frac{1}{20}$ or 0.95. Referring to Table II, we find that the proper value of T is $T = 1.96$. Therefore, after calculating σ for the set of observations, we should discard any observation whose deviation from the mean is larger than 1.96σ.

Table III is a short tabulation of maximum values of $T = d_i/\sigma$ which should be tolerated, according to Chauvenet's criterion. For example, with 20 observations, the maximum value of T is 2.24. If σ for a set of 20 voltage measurements is 0.01 volt, then any observation deviating from the mean by more than 2.24×0.01 volt $= 0.0224$ volt should be discarded.

If we eliminate an observation by Chauvenet's criterion, we should eliminate it *completely*. This means that after the anomalous observations are eliminated, we must recompute the mean and the standard deviation using the remaining observations. If one decides to use Chauvenet's criterion, it should be kept in mind that it may be possible to eliminate most or all of the data by repeated applications. Thus the criterion, of dubious validity at best even on the first round, should certainly not be used more than once.

Between the two extreme views just presented, there are other more moderate views on rejection of data. Some of these unquestionably have better theoretical justification than Chauvenet's criterion. They are also more complicated to use. We shall outline qualitatively one method which is sometimes used.[1]

If there are more observations in the "tails" of

[1] For a full discussion of this method, see H. Jeffreys, "Theory of Probability," sec. 4.41, Oxford University Press, New York, 1948.

the distribution than seems reasonable, one might suspect that the distribution is not quite normal; it may be approximately a Gauss distribution near the mean but somewhat larger than Gaussian in the tails. We can make some simple assumption regarding the small modification to be made in the distribution to represent probabilities for large deviations in agreement with the observations. Then we use the principle of maximum likelihood, which will be used for the theory of least squares in Sec. 14, to determine the most probable value of the observed quantity. This turns out to be a weighted mean, in which the observations far from the mean are given considerably less weight than those in the center. This procedure involves a fair amount of computation, but it is undoubtedly more honest than Chauvenet's criterion.

11 | Goodness of Fit

We now return briefly to a question raised at the end of Sec. 6; that is, if we suspect that a given set of observations comes from some particular parent distribution, how can we test them for agreement with this distribution?

Consider the example of Sec. 6, the probability distribution for the results of rolling two dice. The probability distribution $f(n)$ tabulated on page 41 is computed on the assumption that each die is symmetric, so that the six numbers on each are all equally likely.

Now we roll the dice a large number of times, recording the totals. It is not very likely that 12 will occur on *exactly* $\frac{1}{36}$ of the trials, but we expect the result to be close to $\frac{1}{36}$. If it turns out to be $\frac{1}{2}$ instead, there is probably something very strange about these dice. Now, the problem is: How much disagreement between the parent distribution (in this case the table on page 41) and our sample distribution can we reasonably expect, if the sample *is* taken from this parent distribution? Or, to put the question another way, how great must the disagreement be in order to justify the conclusion that the dice do *not* obey the parent distribution (i.e., that they are loaded)?

What we need is a quantitative index of the difference in the two distributions, and a means of interpreting this index. The sample distribution is expressed most naturally in terms of the *frequencies* of the various events, where the frequency of an event is defined as the total number of times this event occurs among all the trials. Thus it is convenient to express our distributions in terms of frequencies rather than probabilities. Specifically, let $F(n)$ be the frequency of event n (in this case, simply the occurrence of the total n) for the sample, which we shall assume to consist of N trials. If the parent distribution which we are comparing with this sample is $f(n)$, then the frequency predicted by the parent distribution is just $Nf(n)$. The difference $Nf(n) - F(n)$ for each n characterizes the difference in the two frequencies.

The most widely used test for comparing the sample and parent frequencies (or for examining the "goodness of fit" of the sample) consists of computing a weighted mean of the square of the fractional difference of the two frequencies. The resulting quantity is called χ^2; this quantity, together with a suitable interpretation, constitutes the "χ^2 test of goodness of fit."

The quantity $[Nf(n) - F(n)]/Nf(n)$ represents the fractional difference in the frequencies for a given n. Our first impulse is to square this quantity and sum over n. A little thought shows, however, that this would weight the "tails" of the distribution, whose statistical fluctuations are always relatively large, as much as the center. Thus a better criterion for goodness of fit is obtained by multiplying by a weighting factor $Nf(n)$, which then weights the fractional difference according to the importance of the event n in the distribution. Thus it is customary to define a measure of goodness of fit called χ^2 by the equation

$$\chi^2 = \sum_n \frac{[Nf(n) - F(n)]^2}{Nf(n)} \tag{11.1}$$

This discussion is not intended to be a thorough exposition of the reasons for this particular definition of χ^2. To give such an exposition we should relate χ^2 to the idea of the least-squares sum which is introduced in Sec. 14. Such a discussion is beyond the scope of this book; instead, we simply recognize that Eq. (11.1) seems intuitively to be a reasonable index of goodness of fit.

There remains the question of how to interpret the result of Eq. (11.1). Clearly, if the sample distribution and the assumed parent distribution agree exactly, then $\chi^2 = 0$. This is of course extremely unlikely; even if the sample *is* taken from the assumed parent distribution, one would not expect *exact* agreement in every interval. But, the larger χ^2 is, the more disagreement there is between the two distributions. The proper question to ask is: How large a value of χ^2 is reasonable if the sample *is* taken from the assumed parent? If we obtain a value of χ^2 larger than this reasonable value, then we should assume that the sample *does not* agree with the parent.

Calculating values of χ^2 which can occur simply by chance is quite involved, and we cannot discuss the problem here. Instead, we give a short table which will help interpret χ^2 in specific situations. Table IV lists values of χ^2 for which the probability of occurrence of a χ^2 *larger* than this is a given value P, assuming that the sample *is* taken from the parent distribution used in computing χ^2. This value depends on the number of points at which the theoretical and sample frequencies are compared, which is called ν in the table.

In the dice-rolling example, we are comparing the two frequencies for 11 different events; so in this case $\nu = 11$. For $\nu = 11$, the table lists the value $\chi^2 = 6.989$

under $P = 0.80$, and the value $\chi^2 = 24.725$ under $P = 0.01$. This means that if the sample "fits" the assumed parent distribution, there is an 80% chance that χ^2 will be 6.989 or larger, because of random fluctuations, but only a 1% chance that it will be greater than 24.725. Thus if we calculate χ^2 for a sample and obtain a value around 7, we can say that this is probably due to chance fluctuations, and the sample *does* fit the assumed parent. If on the other hand we obtain $\chi^2 = 40$, then it is very unlikely that this value occurred by chance, and the sample probably *does not* fit the parent. Note that the χ^2 test never gives a cut-and-dried answer "it fits" or "it does not fit." Some judgment is required in all cases.

It is not necessary that the frequencies refer to individual events. They may just as well refer to *groups* of events. Suppose, for example, that we are observing radioactive decays and want to compare the distribution of the number of events in a given time interval with the Poisson distribution with a given value of a. In a particular case it might be expedient to consider the following four groups: $n = 0$; $n = 1$; $n = 2$, 3, or 4; $n > 4$. For these four groups we have four comparisons between the sample and parent frequencies. In this case, then, $\nu = 4$.

An additional complication arises if we must determine the quantity a from the sample distribution. It can be shown that the most probable value of a from the sample is simply the mean of the sample distribution, as we might have guessed from Eq. (8.6). But in using the sample to determine a, we have *forced* a certain degree of agreement between the two frequencies. Thus the number of real comparisons is reduced from four to three, and we should use $\nu = 3$.

In general, when comparing a sample with a parent distribution using K groups of events, we take $\nu = K$ if the parameters of the parent distribution (such as a for the Poisson distribution, or N and p for the binomial) are specified in advance. If one parameter of the parent distribution (such as a) is determined from the sample, we take $\nu = K - 1$; if two parameters (such as N and p) are determined from the sample, we take $\nu = K - 2$, and so on.

It is easy to extend this method to the case where the observed quantity, say x, is a continuous variable, so that the parent distribution $f(x)$ is a function of a continuous variable. We divide the range of values of x into a series of nonoverlapping intervals which together cover the whole range. Call a typical interval Δx_k, and the value of x at its center x_k. Assume that there are K intervals in all, so that k ranges from 1 to K. The probability P_k given by the parent distribution for a measurement to fall in this interval is

$$P_k = \int_{x_k - \Delta x_k/2}^{x_k + \Delta x_k/2} f(x)\, dx \tag{11.2}$$

In usual practice, the intervals are sufficiently small, except perhaps in the "tails" of the distribution, so that this integral can be approximated by taking the value of $f(x)$ at the center and multiplying by the width of the interval; this is equivalent to assuming that $f(x)$ is approximately constant over any single interval. In this case, we have approximately

$$P_k = f(x_k)\Delta x_k \tag{11.3}$$

The frequency predicted by the parent distribution is then NP_k; the sample frequency F_k is of course the number of times the variable x falls in the interval Δx_k in the given sample. In this case the appropriate definition of χ^2 is

$$\chi^2 = \sum_{k=1}^{K} \frac{(NP_k - F_k)^2}{NP_k} \tag{11.4}$$

PROBLEMS

1. Six pennies are tossed simultaneously. What are the probabilities for *no* heads? One head? Two? Three? Four? Five? Six? ??? ? Would the probabilities be the same if, instead, one penny was tossed six times? Explain.

2. One die (singular of dice) is rolled. What is the probability that 6 will come up? If four dice are rolled, what is the probability for *no* 6s? One? Two? Three? Four? Five?

3. Among a large number of eggs, 1% were found to be rotten. In a dozen eggs, what is the probability that none is rotten? One? More than one?

4. A man starts out for a Sunday afternoon walk, playing the following game. At the starting point he tosses a coin. If the result is heads, he walks north one block; if tails, south one block. Find all the possible positions after four tosses, and the probability for each.

5. In Prob. 4, derive the probability distribution for the possible positions after N tosses of the coin.

6. In Prob. 5, if the man walks on several different Sundays, what is the *average* distance he reaches from the starting point after N tosses? What is the *standard deviation* of his positions after N tosses?

7. The man plays the same game as in Prob. 4, but instead of tossing one coin he tosses two. If *both* are heads, he walks a block north; for any other result he walks a block south. Find the possible positions after four tosses, and the probability for each.

8. In Prob. 7, derive the probability distribution for the possible positions after N tosses of the coin.

9. Answer the questions asked in Prob. 6, for the distribution obtained in Prob. 8.

10. The scores in a final examination were found to be distributed according to the following table:

Score	Distribution, %	Score	Distribution, %
95–100	4	65–69	14
90– 94	6	60–64	10
85– 89	8	55–59	6
80– 84	12	50–54	2
75– 79	16	40–49	2
70– 74	18	9–39	2

a. Draw a histogram illustrating this distribution.

b. Calculate approximate values for the mean and variance of the distribution.

c. If 15% of the students failed the examination, what was the lowest passing grade?

11. Observations on 200 litters of cocker spaniel puppies revealed the following statistics:

Litters	Puppies in each litter
5	4
17	5
34	6
47	7
31	8
25	9
18	10
14	11
7	12
2	13

Find the mean number in a litter, and the standard deviation.

12. A lump of Shakespeareum (a fictitious radioactive element) contains 10^{21} nuclei. The probability that any one will decay in 10 sec is found to be 2×10^{-21}. Find the probability that in a given 10-sec period *no* decays will occur. Also one decay, two, three, etc. Find the number of decays per 10 sec such that the probability of *more* decays than this number is less than 0.1%. The answer to this part will determine what is meant by "etc." in the first part.

13. A group of underfed chickens were observed for 50 consecutive days and found to lay the following numbers of eggs:

Eggs laid	No. of days
0	10
1	13
2	13
3	8
4	4
5	2

Show that this is approximately a Poisson distribution. Calculate the mean and standard deviation directly from the data. Compare with standard deviation predicted by the Poisson distribution.

14. Derive Eq. (8.6) for the *mean* of the Poisson distribution directly from Eqs. (6.2) and (8.5). To evaluate the sum, insert Eq. (8.5) into Eq. (8.7) and differentiate the result with respect to a. This procedure is similar to that used in Appendix B for the binomial distribution.

15. Derive Eq. (8.9) for the variance of the Poisson distribution directly from Eqs. (6.4) and (8.5) by the same procedure suggested in Prob. 14.

16. During a summer shower which lasted 10 min, 10^6 raindrops fell on a square area 10 m on a side. The top of a convertible was actuated by a rain-sensing element 1 cm square; so the interior of the car was protected in case of rain.

   a. Find the probability that at least one raindrop landed on the element.

   b. In such a shower how much time must elapse after the shower begins, on the average, before the top closes itself?

17. It has been observed in human reproduction that twins occur approximately once in 100 births. If the number of babies in a birth follows a Poisson distribution, calculate the probability of the birth of quintuplets. Do you think it likely that octuplets have ever been born in the history of man?

18. A coin is tossed 10,000 times; the results are 5176 heads and 4824 tails. Is this a reasonable result for a symmetric coin, or is it fairly conclusive evidence that the coin is asymmetric? (*Hint:* Calculate the total probability for *more* than 5176 heads in 10,000 tosses. To do this, approximate

the binomial distribution by a Gauss distribution, as discussed in the last paragraph of Appendix C.)

19. Calculate the mean deviation for the Gauss distribution. Express your result as a multiple of σ.

20. If a set of measurements is distributed according to the Gauss distribution, find the probability that any single measurement will fall between $(m - \frac{1}{2}\sigma)$ and $(m + \frac{1}{2}\sigma)$.

21. The "probable error" of a distribution is defined as the error such that the probability of occurrence of an error whose absolute value is less than this value is $\frac{1}{2}$. Find the probable error for the normal (Gauss) distribution, and express it as a multiple of σ. Is this *the most probable error?* If not, what is?

22. Show that the graph representing the results of Prob. 1 can be approximated by a normal distribution curve. Find the appropriate mean and standard deviation for this curve.

23. Consider the data of Prob. 27. If these are normally distributed, and if two additional measurements are made, find:

a. The probability that *both* will be in the interval 54.98 to 55.02 cm.

b. The probability that *neither* will be in this interval.

24. The measurements (x) in a certain experiment are distributed according to the function

$F(x) = A/[(x - m)^2 + b^2]$.

a. Sketch the function.

b. Find the value of A needed to normalize the function.

c. What is the mean of the distribution?

d. Discuss the standard deviation of the distribution.

25. Suppose that the function of Prob. 24 were "cut off" at $x = m \pm b$. That is, $F(x)$ is the given function in the inter-

val $m - b < x < m + b$, but $F(x) = 0$ for values outside this interval. Answer the questions of Prob. 24.

26. An object undergoes simple harmonic motion with amplitude A and frequency f according to the equation $x = A \sin 2\pi ft$, where x represents the displacement from equilibrium. Calculate the mean and standard deviation of the position and of the speed of the object.

27. The height of a mercury column in a manometer was measured using a cathetometer. The following measurements were obtained:

cm	cm
55.06	54.99
54.92	55.02
55.01	55.03
55.00	55.02
54.98	54.97

Test these data using Chauvenet's criterion to determine which should be discarded. After discarding the appropriate data, recompute the mean. By how much does it differ from the original mean? Compare this difference with σ for the set of data.

28. Apply the χ^2 test to the data of Prob. 13.

29. Discuss how the χ^2 test might be applied in Prob. 18.

CHAPTER IV

FURTHER DEVELOPMENTS

All that has been said so far about probability and probability distributions has established a foundation on which we can now build several techniques of great practical importance in handling experimental data. This chapter contains several very powerful tools which are developed from the principles we have learned so far.

12 | Standard Deviation of the Mean

We return to an important question which was raised in Sec. 3. This is: What is the relation between the standard deviation of a set of measurements and the precision of the *mean* of the set?

We answer this question by a straightforward extension of the ideas which have already been introduced. First, suppose that we take N measurements having random errors which follow the Gauss distribution. We calculate the mean and σ of this set of measurements. Now suppose we take *another* set of N measurements and calculate the mean and σ of this set. This mean will not in general be exactly equal to the mean of the first set, although we expect intuitively that the difference of the means on the average will be considerably smaller than the difference between the individual measurements. The values of σ will be somewhat different also. Another way of saying the same thing is to say that the mean and variance of a *sample* of N observations are not in general equal to the mean and variance of the parent distribution. We continue this process until we have taken many sets, say M, each with its own mean and σ. We now ask: What is the *standard deviation of the means?* It is clear that this standard deviation provides an indication of how reliable any one of the means is.

To facilitate our calculation of the standard deviation of the means, for which we shall use the symbol σ_m, we introduce some new notation. We shall take M sets of measurements with N measurements in each set. There will then be MN readings in all. We use a Greek index μ to indicate which set of measurements we are talking about and i, as always, to designate a particular measurement within a set. Let

$x_{\mu i}$ = measurement i in set μ

$\bar{x}_\mu$ = mean of set μ

$\overline{X}$ = mean of all measurements

$d_{\mu i} = x_{\mu i} - \overline{X}$ = deviation of $x_{\mu i}$

$D_\mu = \bar{x}_\mu - \overline{X}$ = deviation of mean $\bar{x}_\mu$

The variance of the individual measurements is given by

$$\sigma^2 = \frac{1}{MN} \sum_{\mu=1}^{M} \sum_{i=1}^{N} d_{\mu i}{}^2 \tag{12.1}$$

The variance of the means is given by

$$\sigma_m{}^2 = \frac{1}{M} \sum_{\mu=1}^{M} D_\mu{}^2 \tag{12.2}$$

Now the deviations D_μ of the means can be expressed in terms of the deviations $d_{\mu i}$ of the individual observations, as follows:

$$D_\mu = \bar{x}_\mu - \bar{X} = \frac{1}{N} \sum_{i=1}^{N} x_{\mu i} - \bar{X}$$

$$= \frac{1}{N} \sum_{i=1}^{N} (x_{\mu i} - \bar{X}) = \frac{1}{N} \sum_{i=1}^{N} d_{\mu i} \tag{12.3}$$

Inserting Eq. (12.3) into Eq. (12.2), we obtain

$$\sigma_m{}^2 = \frac{1}{M} \sum_{\mu=1}^{M} \left(\frac{1}{N} \sum_{i=1}^{N} d_{\mu i} \right)^2 = \frac{1}{MN^2} \sum_{\mu=1}^{M} \left(\sum_{i=1}^{N} d_{\mu i} \right)^2 \tag{12.4}$$

Now let us squint for a moment at Eq. (12.4). The double sum at the right side of this equation, when evaluated, contains two different kinds of terms. There are terms in which one of the $d_{\mu i}$ is squared, and other terms containing products of two different $d_{\mu i}$. Now, because of the symmetry of the Gauss distribution function with respect to positive and negative deviations, the ds are as likely to be positive as negative. So in the limit, when we take a very large set of observations

MN, the products of two different ds will tend to cancel each other out. In Eq. (12.4) it is therefore legitimate to replace

$$\sum_{\mu=1}^{M} \left(\sum_{i=1}^{N} d_{\mu i} \right)^2 \qquad \text{by} \qquad \sum_{\mu=1}^{M} \sum_{i=1}^{N} d_{\mu i}^2$$

which contains only the d^2 terms. This argument for eliminating the cross terms is intended to be a plausibility argument rather than a rigorous one. It is quite possible but somewhat involved to put it on a more firm mathematical basis.

Equation (12.4) now becomes

$$\sigma_m^2 = \frac{1}{MN^2} \sum_{\mu=1}^{M} \sum_{i=1}^{N} d_{\mu i}^2 \tag{12.5}$$

This is closely related to Eq. (12.1). Combining Eq. (12.1) and Eq. (12.5), we obtain

$$\sigma_m^2 = \frac{\sigma^2}{N} \qquad \text{or} \qquad \sigma_m = \frac{\sigma}{\sqrt{N}} \tag{12.6}$$

The variance of the *mean* of a set of N measurements is simply the variance of the individual measurements divided by the number of measurements!

The standard deviation of the mean is used universally to describe the precision of the *mean* of the set of measurements; we now have available a method of *calculating* the standard deviation of the mean from the measurements themselves. In the surveyor's problem at the end of Sec. 9, for example, we find that the standard deviation of the mean is $0.026 \text{ ft}/\sqrt{10} = 0.008$ ft. There is about a 68% chance that the mean is within 0.008 ft of the mean of the parent distribution, which is presumably the true value of the quantity.

A word of caution about Eq. (12.6) is in order. It should not be thought that this equation is valid for measurements taken from *every* parent distribution. We have assumed that the cross terms in the sum used to find σ_m^2 are negligibly small. This is true for the Gauss distribution, as may be proved from a theorem known as the *central limit theorem*. Because experimental measurements so often obey the Gauss distribution, this is a useful formula. But it is quite possible to dream up strange distributions for which Eq. (12.6) is not true. For the Cauchy distribution, which will not be discussed here, σ_m^2 may be infinite!

13 | Propagation of Errors

We now return to the question raised in Sec. 2—the effect which errors in measurements have on the error of the result of a calculation which incorporates these measurements. We consider a quantity Q which is to be calculated from several observed quantities $a, b, c, \ldots$:

$$Q = f(a, b, c, \ldots) \tag{13.1}$$

Suppose that $a, b, c, \ldots$ are all measured N times. We can then calculate N different values of Q. We can also calculate the mean and variance for the set of measurements of a,

$$\sigma_a{}^2 = \frac{1}{N} \sum_{i=1}^{N} (\Delta a_i)^2 \tag{13.2}$$

where $\Delta a_i = a_i - \bar{a}$, and also the variance of Q,

$$\sigma_Q{}^2 = \frac{1}{N} \sum_{i=1}^{N} (\Delta Q_i)^2 \tag{13.3}$$

where $\overline{Q} = f(\bar{a}, \bar{b}, \ldots)$, $Q_i = f(a_i, b_i, \ldots)$, and $\Delta Q_i = Q_i - \overline{Q}$. The ΔQ_i can be approximated by the same methods used in Sec. 2, Eq. (2.8):

$$\Delta Q_i \cong \frac{\partial Q}{\partial a} \Delta a_i + \frac{\partial Q}{\partial b} \Delta b_i + \cdots \tag{13.4}$$

Inserting Eq. (13.4) into Eq. (13.3),

$$\sigma_Q{}^2 = \frac{1}{N} \sum_{i=1}^{N} \left(\frac{\partial Q}{\partial a} \Delta a_i + \frac{\partial Q}{\partial b} \Delta b_i + \cdots \right)^2 \tag{13.5}$$

When the quantity in the parentheses in Eq. (13.5) is squared, two kinds of terms appear. The first are squares, a typical one of which is

$$\left(\frac{\partial Q}{\partial a} \Delta a_i \right)^2$$

The other terms are cross terms of the form

$$\frac{\partial Q}{\partial a} \frac{\partial Q}{\partial b} \Delta a_i \, \Delta b_i$$

Now, we use exactly the same argument as used in Sec. 12 to obtain Eq. (12.5). The cross terms, since they contain quantities which are equally likely to be positive or negative, add up to very nearly zero, or at least something very much smaller than the sum of the squared terms. We therefore drop them from the sum; the remaining terms are

$$\sigma_Q{}^2 = \frac{1}{N} \sum_{i=1}^{N} \left[\left(\frac{\partial Q}{\partial a}\right)^2 (\Delta a_i)^2 + \left(\frac{\partial Q}{\partial b}\right)^2 (\Delta b_i)^2 + \cdots \right]$$

(13.6)

This can be rewritten:

$$\sigma_Q{}^2 = \left(\frac{\partial Q}{\partial a}\right)^2 \frac{1}{N} \sum_{i=1}^{N} \Delta a_i{}^2 + \left(\frac{\partial Q}{\partial b}\right)^2 \frac{1}{N} \sum_{i=1}^{N} \Delta b_i{}^2 + \cdots$$

$$= \left(\frac{\partial Q}{\partial a}\right)^2 \sigma_a{}^2 + \left(\frac{\partial Q}{\partial b}\right)^2 \sigma_b{}^2 + \cdots \qquad (13.7)$$

This important result gives us a relation between the variances of the individual observations and the variance of the quantity Q calculated from these observations.

Usually, we are interested not in the variance of the individual observations, but in the variance of the *mean*. Assuming that the errors are normally distributed, we can convert Eq. (13.7) into one containing variances of the means by using Eq. (12.6). The result is

$$\sigma_{mQ}{}^2 = \left(\frac{\partial Q}{\partial a}\right)^2 \sigma_{ma}{}^2 + \left(\frac{\partial Q}{\partial b}\right)^2 \sigma_{mb}{}^2 + \cdots \qquad (13.8)$$

where $\sigma_{mQ}{}^2$ is the variance of the mean of Q, $\sigma_{ma}{}^2$ the variance of the mean of a, and so forth.

This is the result referred to at the end of Sec. 2; it is of much greater usefulness than Eq. (2.8) because it is the correct formula to use when the standard deviations of the means of a, b, . . . are known. The corresponding formula for the fractional standard deviation of the mean, obtained by simply dividing Eq. (13.8) by Q^2, is

$$\left(\frac{\sigma_{mQ}}{Q}\right)^2 = \left(\frac{1}{Q}\frac{\partial Q}{\partial a}\right)^2 \sigma_{ma}{}^2 + \left(\frac{1}{Q}\frac{\partial Q}{\partial b}\right) \sigma_{mb}{}^2 + \cdots$$

(13.9)

A further remark needs to be made concerning Eq. (13.8), the truth of which is not exhibited clearly by the nonrigorous derivation which we have given. Equation (13.8) can be shown to be true even if *different numbers of observations* are made on the quantities a, b, c. So Eq. (13.8) actually has a much wider range of applicability than has been demonstrated. In the case of unequal numbers of observations, however, Eq. (13.7) must be modified, and the derivation of Eq. (13.8) is a little more involved. In what follows we shall make use of this more general validity of Eq. (13.8), although the proof has not been given here.

Here is an example of the foregoing analysis. Suppose the quantity Q is the area of a rectangle, whose dimensions are a and b; then $Q = ab$. Using Eq. (13.8), we find

$$\sigma_Q{}^2 = b^2\sigma_a{}^2 + a^2\sigma_b{}^2$$

(13.10)

In Eq. (13.10) and in the remainder of this section the subscript m is dropped from the standard deviations, but it is understood that each standard deviation is that of the *mean*, unless otherwise noted. Thus, σ_a is the standard deviation of the *mean* of a.

Introducing the *fractional* standard deviations of the means, σ_a/a, etc., we obtain

$$\left(\frac{\sigma_Q}{Q}\right)^2 = \left(\frac{\sigma_a}{a}\right)^2 + \left(\frac{\sigma_b}{b}\right)^2 \tag{13.11}$$

More generally, if $Q = a^m b^n$, then it is easy to show that

$$\left(\frac{\sigma_Q}{Q}\right)^2 = m^2\left(\frac{\sigma_a}{a}\right)^2 + n^2\left(\frac{\sigma_b}{b}\right)^2 \tag{13.12}$$

This Pythagorean sort of addition of fractional standard deviations makes them very convenient for practical calculations.

It is important to note the difference between Eq. (13.8) derived in this section and the much more naïve result, Eq. (2.8). If even crude estimates of the standard deviations of the means of the measurements are available, Eq. (13.8) *always* gives a more reliable estimate of the precision of the result than Eq. (2.8); therefore Eq. (13.8) should always be used in such cases. Only if the actual errors are known is Eq. (2.8) used.

Here is an example of the methods developed in this section. Suppose we have a horizontal beam of length l, supported at its ends and loaded in the center with a weight w. It can be shown that the deflection Y at the center of the beam is given by

$$Y = \frac{wl^3}{48EI}$$

where E is an elastic modulus and I is the moment of inertia of the cross section about its center of area.

Now it may happen that the characteristics of the

beam, E and I, are known very well, but that one has only crude measurements of w and l:

$$w = 100 \text{ tons} \pm 1 \text{ ton}$$
$$l = \ \ 50 \text{ ft} \pm 0.5 \text{ ft}$$

where the "$\pm$" in each case refers to the standard deviation of the mean. What is the resulting fractional standard deviation of Y? This is just the question answered by Eq. (13.12). We have

$$\left(\frac{\sigma_Y}{Y}\right)^2 = \left(\frac{\sigma_w}{w}\right)^2 + 3^2\left(\frac{\sigma_l}{l}\right)^2$$

$$= (0.01)^2 + 3^2(0.01)^2 = 0.001$$

$$\frac{\sigma_Y}{Y} = 0.032$$

Note that although w and l have equal fractional standard deviations, σ_l has a much more important effect because l appears to the third power. Also, the fractional standard deviation in Y is considerably larger than that in either w or l.

14 | Method of Least Squares

We now come to a very powerful method for obtaining the most reliable possible information from a set of experimental observations. We first state the *principle of least squares* for a set of measurements on one quantity, and then discuss how the principle can be derived from the *principle of maximum likelihood* if the errors follow the

Gauss distribution. In the next section we discuss applications of the principle to observations of more than one unknown quantity.

The principle of least squares can be stated as follows: The most probable value of a quantity is obtained from a set of measurements by choosing the value which minimizes the sum of the squares of the deviations of these measurements. For a set of measurements x_i the most probable value of x is that which minimizes the quantity

$$\sum_{i=1}^{N} (x - x_i)^2 \tag{14.1}$$

in which x is regarded as a variable which can be varied to obtain the minimum value of the function (14.1).

We note in passing that expression (14.1) is just N times the variance of the x_i, computed on the basis of the most probable value x. Thus an equivalent statement of the principle of least squares is: The most probable value of a quantity is that value which minimizes the variance (or alternately the standard deviation) of the measurements.

We know that the condition which must be satisfied for the function (14.1) to be a minimum is

$$\frac{d}{dx} \sum_{i=1}^{N} (x - x_i)^2 = 0 \tag{14.2}$$

This is a derivative of a sum of terms; we evaluate it by differentiating each term in turn:

$$\frac{d}{dx} \sum_{i=1}^{N} (x - x_i)^2 = \sum_{i=1}^{N} \frac{d}{dx}(x - x_i)^2$$

$$= \sum_{1=i}^{N} 2(x - x_i) = 2Nx - 2 \sum_{i=1}^{N} x_i \quad (14.3)$$

The condition which must be satisfied is therefore

$$2Nx - 2 \sum_{i=1}^{N} x_i = 0$$

or

$$x = \frac{1}{N} \sum_{i=1}^{N} x_i \quad (14.4)$$

The proper value of x to use is just the average of the observations! This is the result which we *guessed* to be correct in Sec. 3.

Now, why should it be desirable to minimize the sum of the squares of the deviations? To answer this question, let us consider first the probability of occurrence of the set of measurements x_i which we obtained. Assuming that the measurements are distributed normally (according to the Gauss distribution), the probability of obtaining a measurement within an interval dx of x_i is

$$P_i = \frac{1}{\sigma\sqrt{2\pi}} e^{-(x-x_i)^2/2\sigma^2} \, dx \quad (14.5)$$

where σ characterizes the parent distribution from which x_i is obtained. The probability of obtaining the whole set of N measurements is the *product* of the separate probabilities:

$$P = P_1 P_2 \cdots P_N$$

$$= \left(\frac{1}{\sigma\sqrt{2\pi}}\, e^{-(x-x_1)^2/2\sigma^2}\, dx \right)$$

$$\cdots \left(\frac{1}{\sigma\sqrt{2\pi}}\, e^{-(x-x_N)^2/2\sigma^2}\, dx \right)$$

$$= \left(\frac{dx}{\sigma\sqrt{2\pi}} \right)^N \exp\left[-\sum_{i=1}^{N} (x - x_i)^2/2\sigma^2 \right] \quad (14.6)$$

Now the plot is beginning to thicken! The probability P of observing the whole set of measurements x_i depends upon the value of x, of course. If x is a number vastly different from any of the x_i, then the exponent in the last form of Eq. (14.6) is a very large negative quantity, and P will be very small. That is, it is very unlikely that we obtain a set of measurements *all* of which are very far from the true value of the quantity.

We now make a basic assumption, called the *principle of maximum likelihood;* we assume that the set of measurements which we obtain is actually *the most probable* set of measurements. According to this assumption, the proper value of x to choose is that which gives P the largest possible value. We want to *maximize* the probability of obtaining the particular set of measurements which we actually obtained. We then call the value of x so obtained the *most probable value of x.*

Clearly, the way to maximize P is to minimize the

value of the exponent in Eq. (14.6). We shall refer to the sum in this exponent as the *least-squares sum* and denote it by $M(x)$. Thus

$$M(x) = \sum \frac{(x_i - x)^2}{2\sigma^2} \tag{14.7}$$

The principle of maximum likelihood thus leads to the conclusion that we should minimize $M(x)$, which is of course equivalent to minimizing $\sum (x_i - x)^2$, in accordance with our original statement.

To summarize what has been said so far: We have assumed that the best value of the observed quantity which we can obtain is the value which maximizes the probability of the set of observations which we have obtained, and we have called this the *most probable value*. If the observations are distributed normally, we maximize the probability by minimizing the sum of the squares of the deviations. For the case of observations on one quantity, this leads to the conclusion that the most probable value of the observed quantity is simply the arithmetic mean of the series of observations. Saying the same thing in slightly different language, we want to find the mean of the infinite parent distribution, which we regard as the true value of the quantity. The best estimate we can make of this mean is the mean of the sample of N measurements.

The standard deviation of the most probable value of x obtained above can be found easily by using the propagation of errors formula, Eq. (13.8). The quantity x is regarded as a function of all the x_i, each of which has a standard deviation equal to that of the parent distribution, that is, σ. Therefore,

$$\sigma_m{}^2 = \left(\frac{\partial x}{\partial x_1}\right)^2 \sigma^2 + \left(\frac{\partial x}{\partial x_2}\right)^2 \sigma^2 + \cdots = \sum_{i=1}^{N} \left(\frac{\partial x}{\partial x_i}\right)^2 \sigma^2$$

$$(14.8)$$

From Eq. (14.4) we find

$$\frac{\partial x}{\partial x_i} = \frac{1}{N} \tag{14.9}$$

so

$$\sigma_m{}^2 = \sum \frac{\sigma^2}{N^2} = \frac{\sigma^2}{N} \tag{14.10}$$

This result should not be surprising; it is the same conclusion we reached in Sec. 12, Eq. (12.6), from a slightly different point of view. The difference between Eq. (14.10) and Eq. (12.6) is that Eq. (14.10) contains the variance of the infinite parent distribution, while Eq. (12.6) contains the variance of a sample of N measurements, which is used as an *estimate* of the variance of the parent distribution. The error of this estimate is thrown away when we discard the cross terms in Eq. (12.4).

The variance of the parent distribution is of course not known. All that can be done is to estimate it by computing the variance of the sample, and this is ordinarily sufficient. In extremely critical work it is occasionally desirable to inquire into the precision of the sample variance, that is, to ask how well it is likely to approximate the variance of the parent distribution.

This can be investigated in a straightforward way by computing the variance *of the variance*. We shall not discuss this calculation here; it is rarely needed.

In the foregoing discussion we have assumed that all the x_i belong to the same infinite parent distribution and that this is a normal distribution. But one can easily think of cases where this is not true. If one makes a series of measurements with an ordinary meter stick, and then measures with a good-quality steel scale, the random errors will in general be distributed differently in the two cases. There may of course also be systematic errors; we assume here that these have been either eliminated or corrected.

How shall we handle the case when the x_i come from different parent distributions? Specifically, suppose that x_i comes from a normal parent distribution characterized by variance σ_i^2. Referring to Eq. (14.6), we see that the probability of the set of measurements must be written as

$$P = \frac{(dx)^N}{\sigma_1 \sigma_2 \cdots \sigma_N (\sqrt{2\pi})^N} \exp\left[-\sum \frac{(x - x_i)^2}{2\sigma_i^2} \right]$$

$$(14.11)$$

The "least-squares sum" in this case is $\sum (x - x_i)^2 / 2\sigma_i^2$. To maximize P, according to the principle of maximum likelihood, we minimize this sum, leading to the condition

$$\frac{d}{dx} \sum \frac{(x - x_i)^2}{2\sigma_i^2} = 0 \qquad (14.12)$$

Carrying out the differentiation and rearranging the result, we find

$$x = \frac{\Sigma \, x_i/\sigma_i^2}{\Sigma \, 1/\sigma_i^2} \tag{14.13}$$

We have found that the most probable value of x in this case is not the simple mean of the x_i, but a *weighted mean*, in which each weight w_i is the reciprocal of the variance of the corresponding parent distribution.

We have thus obtained an important and very useful result: In computing the average of several quantities whose variances are known, the most probable value is a weighted average in which each weight w_i is given by

$$w_i = \frac{1}{\sigma_i^2} \tag{14.14}$$

The variance of the value of x obtained from Eq. (14.13) can be found by exactly the same procedure used to derive Eq. (14.10). From the propagation-of-errors formula, Eq. (13.8), we have, using Eq. (14.14),

$$\sigma_m^2 = \sum_j \left(\frac{\partial x}{\partial x_j}\right)^2 \sigma_j^2 = \sum_j \frac{w_j^2}{\left(\sum_i w_i\right)^2} \sigma_j^2$$

$$= \frac{1}{(\Sigma \, 1/\sigma_i^2)^2} \sum \frac{1}{\sigma_i^2} \tag{14.15}$$

Thus we find

$$\frac{1}{\sigma_m^2} = \sum_i \frac{1}{\sigma_i^2} \tag{14.16}$$

Clearly, the variance of the weighted mean is smaller

than any of the individual variances. We note also that in the special case where all the variances are equal $1/\sigma_m^2 = N/\sigma^2$ and Eq. (14.16) reduces to Eq. (14.10).

As an example of the use of the methods just outlined, suppose that two experimenters have measured the velocity of light in vacuum and have obtained the following results:

1. $c = 299,774 \pm 2$ km/sec
2. $c = 299,778 \pm 4$ km/sec

where the errors are standard deviations of the means. What is the most probable value of c, based on these two determinations, and what is its standard deviation? According to Eq. (14.13), we should weight each observation according to $1/\sigma^2$. Clearly, it is immaterial whether the weights are *equal* to their respective values of $1/\sigma^2$ or simply *proportional* to them. Thus it is correct to give the first determination a weight of 4, and the second a weight of unity. The most probable value is then

$$c = \frac{4 \times 299,774 + 1 \times 299,778}{4 + 1} = 299,774.8 \text{ km/sec}$$

Its standard deviation is given by Eq. (14.16):

$$\frac{1}{\sigma^2} = \frac{1}{(2 \text{ km/sec})^2} + \frac{1}{(4 \text{ km/sec})^2}$$

or

$$\sigma = 1.7 \text{ km/sec}$$

In using Eqs. (14.13) and (14.16), one should keep in mind that the variance associated with each x_i also provides a means of testing whether the values are *consistent* in a statistical sense. Suppose, for example, that on two different days one makes measurements on the melting temperature of a certain alloy. One day's result yields the value $736 \pm 1°C$, and the other day's result is $749 \pm 2°C$, where in each case the figures after the $\pm$ sign are standard deviations. The difference is very much larger than the standard deviation in either result; and the probability of this occurring by chance is infinitesimally small. Thus we suspect that in one or both determinations there is a *systematic* error. Perhaps the composition of the alloy has changed. Considerations of this sort are an important weapon in detecting systematic errors. Of course, one can devise more quantitative tests of consistency; we shall not go into any further detail here.

The result given by Eq. (14.16), and some other results to be derived later, can be obtained somewhat more simply if one is willing to accept a statement which can be put on firm theoretical ground but which we cannot discuss in detail. The statement is this: In Eq. (14.11), which gives the probability of the set of observations as a function of x, P is approximately a *Gauss function of x* if the number of observations is large. That is, P can be represented by

$$P = \text{const} \times e^{-(x-x_0)^2/2\sigma_m^2} \tag{14.17}$$

in which x_0 is the value of x which maximizes P, which we have shown to be equal to the weighted mean, Eq. (14.13), and σ_m^2 is the variance of the mean, which we should like to find. To find $\sigma_m{}^2$, we compare Eq. (14.17) with Eq. (14.11). The sum in Eq. (14.11) is again called the least-squares sum and denoted by $M(x)$. We make a Taylor series expansion of $M(x)$ about the most probable value x_0:

$$M(x) = M(x_0) + (x - x_0)\left(\frac{dM}{dx}\right)_{x_0}$$
$$+ \tfrac{1}{2}(x - x_0)^2\left(\frac{d^2M}{dx^2}\right)_{x_0} + \cdots \qquad (14.18)$$

The derivatives are evaluated at the most probable value, and thus $(dM/dx)_{x_0} = 0$. Comparing Eq. (14.18) with the exponent in Eq. (14.17), we see that they are equal only if

$$\frac{1}{2}\frac{d^2M}{dx^2} = \frac{1}{2\sigma_m{}^2} \qquad (14.19)$$

Thus we conclude that the variance of the mean is related to the least-squares sum by the simple equation

$$\frac{1}{\sigma_m{}^2} = \frac{d^2M}{dx^2} \qquad (14.20)$$

where the derivative is evaluated at the point $x = x_0$. This result can also be used to simplify some derivations in which the maximum likelihood principle is used for the determination of several unknowns.

We conclude this section by considering another application of the method of least squares in a situation slightly different from the simple one of making a series of measurements on a single observable. This example deals instead with determining an unknown quantity indirectly from *pairs* of observations on two other quantities.

Suppose we want to determine the force constant of a spring (or Young's modulus of a wire). Suppose also that there is reason to believe that the spring obeys Hooke's law, so that the relation of force F to elongation y is

$$F = ky \tag{14.21}$$

where k is the spring constant to be determined. We apply several different forces F_i to the spring by hanging accurately calibrated weights on the end. For each, we measure the elongation y_i. The observations are shown graphically in Fig. 14.1.

The y_i all have random errors; we assume that the errors all have the same distribution and thus the same variance. If there were no errors in y_i, we would have $y_i - F_i/k = 0$. As it is, the quantity $d_i = y_i - F_i/k$ represents the error in y_i. Therefore in the principle of maximum likelihood, the correct least-squares sum to use is

$$M(k) = \sum \frac{(y_i - F_i/k)^2}{2\sigma^2} \tag{14.22}$$

Taking dM/dk and setting it equal to zero,

$$\frac{dM}{dk} = \frac{1}{\sigma^2 k^2} \sum F_i(y_i - F_i/k) = 0 \tag{14.23}$$

or

$$k = \frac{\sum F_i^2}{\sum F_i y_i} \tag{14.24}$$

It is enlightening to compare this result with the procedure one might naïvely be tempted to use, namely, the average of the ratios F_i/y_i, or

$$k = \frac{1}{N} \sum \frac{F_i}{y_i}$$

The correct least-squares result, Eq. (14.24), is quite different.

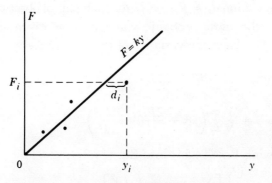

Fig. 14.1. Each point represents a pair of observations of F and y. The deviation d_i corresponding to (F_i, y_i) is shown. The line represents the result of the least-squares calculation.

The variance $\sigma_k{}^2$ of k may be found by use of Eq. (14.20). The derivative of the left side of Eq. (14.23) is d^2M/dk^2; this is

$$\frac{d^2M}{dk^2} = -\frac{2}{\sigma^2 k^3} \sum F_i \left(y_i - \frac{F_i}{k}\right) + \frac{1}{\sigma^2 k^4} \sum F_i{}^2 \quad (14.25)$$

The first sum in this equation is just $(2/k)$ times the first derivative, and this is zero. Thus

$$\frac{1}{\sigma_k{}^2} = \frac{1}{\sigma^2 k^4} \sum_i F_i{}^2 \tag{14.26}$$

The value of k used is, of course, the most probable value just found.

The variance σ^2 of the measurements y_i can be estimated in various ways.

The most straightforward procedure is to compute the deviation $d_i = y_i - F_i/k$ for each pair of observations, using the most probable value of k as given by Eq. (14.24). Then the variance of the y_i is given by

$$\sigma^2 = \frac{1}{N} \sum d_i{}^2$$

$$= \frac{1}{N} \sum \left(y_i{}^2 - \frac{2F_i y_i}{k} + \frac{F_i{}^2}{k^2} \right) \tag{14.27}$$

Inserting Eq. (14.24) into Eq. (14.27),

$$\sigma^2 = \frac{1}{N} \left[\sum y_i{}^2 - \frac{(\Sigma F_i y_i)^2}{\Sigma F_i{}^2} \right]$$

or

$$\sigma^2 = \frac{1}{N} \left(\sum y_i{}^2 - \frac{1}{k} \sum F_i y_i \right) \tag{14.28}$$

Since $\Sigma F_i y_i$ has already been computed, evaluation of Eq. (14.28) involves relatively little additional work. In fact, when such calculations are done by machine, it is usual to compute ΣF_i^2, $\Sigma F_i y_i$, and Σy_i^2 simultaneously.

A direct estimate of σ^2 can be obtained, of course, by repeating the observation several times with the same force. In practical cases, if one wants only a rough estimate of $\sigma_k{}^2$, an estimate or shrewd guess of σ^2, based on inspection of the instruments, may suffice.

15 | Least Squares with Several Unknowns

The method of least squares is also useful when more than one quantity is to be determined from a series of measurements. We start with an example. We know that for an object moving in a straight line with constant acceleration the velocity varies with time according to the relation

$$v = v_0 + at \tag{15.1}$$

where v_0 is the velocity at time $t = 0$. Now suppose that in a particular situation we want to determine the values of v_0 and a by measuring the velocity v_i at each of a succession of times t_i. The measurements might be made, for example, with a speedometer and a stop watch. Furthermore, suppose that the times can be measured very accurately, so that the principal experimental errors are in the velocity measurements.

If we merely measure the velocity at two times, obtaining two pairs of observations (v_1,t_1) and (v_2,t_2), we obtain two simultaneous equations:

$$\begin{aligned} v_1 &= v_0 + at_1 \\ v_2 &= v_0 + at_2 \end{aligned} \tag{15.2}$$

which can be solved to determine v_0 and a. But now suppose that, in order to increase the precision of our results, we take a *series* of pairs of observations, say N

115

pairs in all, of which a typical pair is (v_i, t_i). The resulting set of equations is

$$v_1 = v_0 + at_1$$
$$v_2 = v_0 + at_2 \qquad\qquad (15.3)$$
$$\cdots\cdots\cdots$$
$$v_N = v_0 + at_N$$

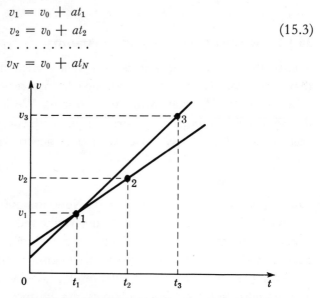

Fig. 15.1. The line which fits observations (v_1, t_1) and (v_2, t_2) has, in general, a different slope (a) and intercept (v_0) from that which fits (v_1, t_1) and (v_3, t_3). There is no straight line which fits all three points.

Now these equations are not in general consistent; if we take different pairs of equations, and solve them for v_0 and a, we obtain different values of v_0 and a. Graphical solutions for v_0 and a are shown in Fig. 15.1. The reason for the various values of v_0 and a, of course, is that there are experimental errors in the v_i. Equations (15.3) should be regarded therefore not as true equalities but as *observation equations* whose two sides are not quite equal. We use the symbol $\overset{\circ}{=}$, which is read "observed to be equal to," and write

$$v_i \overset{\circ}{=} v_0 + at_i \qquad (15.4)$$

In actual fact the two sides of the equation are not exactly equal, but differ by an amount d_i:

$$d_i = v_0 + at_i - v_i \qquad (15.5)$$

where d_i is the deviation corresponding to equation i and the *pair* of observations (v_i, t_i).

Since the d_i are the results of the experimental errors, we shall assume that they are distributed according to the Gauss distribution function. The most probable values of v_0 and a can now be obtained from the principle of maximum likelihood.

For a set of observations (v_i, t_i), they are the values which make this set *most probable*. As in the previous example, this probability is *maximized* when we *minimize* the sum of the squares of the deviations.

Here is the *principle of least squares* operating again. That is, we want to minimize the quantity

$$\Sigma \, d_i^2 = \Sigma \, (v_0 + at_i - v_i)^2 \qquad (15.6)$$

by choosing v_0 and a properly.

To minimize a function of two variables, we take the partial derivative of the function with respect to each of the variables in turn and set each derivative equal to zero. Thus the conditions which determine v_0 and a are

Further Developments

$$\frac{\partial}{\partial v_0} \sum d_i{}^2 = 0 \qquad \text{and} \qquad \frac{\partial}{\partial a} \sum d_i{}^2 = 0 \qquad (15.7)$$

When we evaluate these derivatives, we obtain two equations which then can be solved simultaneously to find v_0 and a. Notice that in general this procedure always gives us as many equations as we have unknown quantities to determine. These equations, of which Eqs. (15.7) are examples, are sometimes called *normal equations*.

Inserting Eq. (15.6) into Eq. (15.7),

$$\frac{\partial}{\partial v_0} \sum d_i{}^2 = \sum 2(v_0 + at_i - v_i) = 0$$

or

$$v_0 N + a \sum t_i = \sum v_i \qquad (15.8a)$$

and

$$\frac{\partial}{\partial a} \sum d_i{}^2 = \sum 2t_i(v_0 + at_i - v_i) = 0$$

or

$$v_0 \sum t_i + a \sum t_i{}^2 = \sum v_i t_i \qquad (15.8b)$$

We now have a pair of simultaneous equations for v_0 and a:

$$\begin{aligned} v_0 N \quad &+ a \Sigma t_i = \Sigma v_i \\ v_0 \Sigma t_i &+ a \Sigma t_i{}^2 = \Sigma v_i t_i \end{aligned} \qquad (15.8)$$

These equations are the *normal equations* for this problem. The number of normal equations is equal to the number of unknowns. Equations (15.8) can be solved in a straightforward manner for v_0 and a, using determinants:

$$v_0 = \frac{\begin{vmatrix} \Sigma\, v_i & \Sigma\, t_i \\ \Sigma\, v_i t_i & \Sigma\, t_i{}^2 \end{vmatrix}}{\begin{vmatrix} N & \Sigma\, t_i \\ \Sigma\, t_i & \Sigma\, t_i{}^2 \end{vmatrix}} = \frac{(\Sigma\, v_i)(\Sigma\, t_i{}^2) - (\Sigma\, v_i t_i)(\Sigma\, t_i)}{N\, \Sigma\, t_i{}^2 - (\Sigma\, t_i)^2}$$

$$\text{(15.9)}$$

$$a = \frac{\begin{vmatrix} N & \Sigma\, v_i \\ \Sigma\, t_i & \Sigma\, v_i t_i \end{vmatrix}}{\begin{vmatrix} N & \Sigma\, t_i \\ \Sigma\, t_i & \Sigma\, t_i{}^2 \end{vmatrix}} = \frac{N\, \Sigma\, v_i t_i - (\Sigma\, v_i)(\Sigma\, t_i)}{N\, \Sigma\, t_i{}^2 - (\Sigma\, t_i)^2}$$

Before proceeding further, it is worthwhile to stop to consider what we have done. If there had not been any experimental errors, all the pairs of observations (v_i, t_i) would have obeyed Eq. (15.1). A graphical rep-

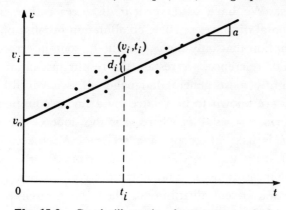

Fig. 15.2. Graph illustrating least-squares calculation of v_0 and a. Each point represents a pair of observations; a typical one is labeled (v_i, t_i), with its deviation. The line is drawn with the values of v_0 and a given by Eqs. (15.9). In general this line need not pass exactly through *any* of the points.

resentation of this statement is that if there were no experimental errors, all the points represented by the coordinates (v_i, t_i) would lie on a straight line whose slope is a and whose intercept on the v axis is v_0. Such a line is shown in Fig. 15.2.

Because of the random errors in the v_i, the actual observations are represented by points which lie somewhat above and below the line, as shown in the figure. Reference to Eq. (15.5), which defines the deviations, shows that the graphical significance of d_i is that its magnitude is the vertical distance between point (v_i, t_i) and the line. The method of least squares selects a line which *minimizes* the sum of squares of these vertical distances. We have used vertical distances rather than horizontal distances or some combination because of the assumption that only the v_i, not the t_i, contain errors.

For reference, we restate the results just obtained, in slightly more general language. If two variables x and y are known to be related by a linear equation of the form $y = mx + b$, where m is the slope of the line and b is its y intercept, if a series of N observations (x_i, y_i) are made, in which random errors occur only in the y_i measurements, and if these errors all belong to the same parent distribution, then the normal equations are

$$
\begin{aligned}
m \, \Sigma \, x_i + bN &= \Sigma \, y_i \\
m \, \Sigma \, x_i^2 + b \, \Sigma \, x_i &= \Sigma x_i y_i
\end{aligned}
\tag{15.10}
$$

and the most probable values of m and b are given by

$$m = \frac{N \sum x_i y_i - (\sum x_i)(\sum y_i)}{N \sum x_i^2 - (\sum x_i)^2}$$

$$b = \frac{(\sum y_i)(\sum x_i^2) - (\sum x_i y_i)(\sum x_i)}{N \sum x_i^2 - (\sum x_i)^2}$$

$$(15.11)$$

These expressions have been obtained directly from Eqs. (15.9) by appropriate substitution of symbols.

The next logical step is to try to calculate the standard deviations of the values of m and b which have been obtained from the method of least squares. This can be done by exactly the same methods as used for the case of one unknown. Errors in m and b are produced by errors in the y_i, which we assume are taken all from the same parent distribution with variance σ^2. Thus we may use Eq. (13.8) to compute the variances of m and b in terms of the variance of the parent distribution. Then the y_i themselves can be used to estimate the variance of the parent distribution.

We proceed as follows: From Eq. (13.8) we obtain

$$\sigma_m^2 = \sum_j \left(\frac{\partial m}{\partial y_j} \right)^2 \sigma^2 \qquad (15.12)$$

The partial derivatives are evaluated by use of Eq. (15.11), in which we abbreviate the denominators by the symbol $\Delta = N \sum x_i^2 - (\sum x_i)^2$. To evaluate

$$\frac{\partial}{\partial y_j} \sum_i x_i y_i$$

we note that there is only one term in the sum in which

121

y_i is the same as y_j, the variable we are differentiating. Therefore,

$$\frac{\partial}{\partial y_j} \sum_i x_i y_i = x_j$$

Similarly,

$$\frac{\partial}{\partial y_j} \sum_i y_i = 1$$

Thus we find

$$\frac{\partial m}{\partial y_j} = \frac{N x_j - \sum x_i}{\Delta} \tag{15.13}$$

$$\left(\frac{\partial m}{\partial y_j}\right)^2 = \frac{N^2 x_j{}^2 - 2N x_j \sum x_i + (\sum x_i)^2}{\Delta^2} \tag{15.14}$$

Inserting Eq. (15.14) into Eq. (15.12),

$$\sigma_m{}^2 = \frac{\sigma^2}{\Delta^2}\left[N^2 \sum x_j{}^2 - 2N\left(\sum x_j\right)\left(\sum x_i\right) + N\left(\sum_i x_i\right)^2\right]$$

$$= \frac{\sigma^2}{\Delta^2}\left[N^2 \sum x_j{}^2 - N\left(\sum x_j\right)^2\right] \tag{15.15}$$

where we have used the obvious fact that $\sum x_i = \sum x_j$. Finally, recalling the definition of Δ,

$$\sigma_m{}^2 = \frac{N \sigma^2}{\Delta} \tag{15.16}$$

Using precisely the same procedure to find the variance of b, we obtain

$$\sigma_b{}^2 = \frac{\sigma^2 \sum x_i{}^2}{\Delta} \tag{15.17}$$

All that remains now is to estimate the variance σ^2

of the parent distribution, and this is easy to do. We recall that the deviation of each observation equation is given by

$$d_i = mx_i + b - y_i \tag{15.18}$$

The variance of the sample is then

$$\sigma^2 = \frac{1}{N} \sum d_i{}^2 = \frac{1}{N} \sum (mx_i + b - y_i)^2 \tag{15.19}$$

in which the values of m and b are those given by Eq. (15.11).

We have now solved, at least *in principle*, the problem of finding the variances of m and b, in that we have shown how they may be computed from the observed data by means of Eqs. (15.16), (15.17), and (15.19). In practice, the calculations are rather long and complicated. For this reason it is important to ask, in any particular problem, whether the variances are needed badly enough to justify the labor of obtaining them. If a large number of data are to be used in an all-out effort to determine constants with the greatest possible precision, then of course one wants to know what the precision is. In this case, the necessary calculations are often done with a high-speed digital computer.

The theory of least squares can be generalized in at least four ways, which we shall discuss only very briefly.

1. It can be used to determine constants in equations when there are more than two unknowns. One has an observation equation for each set of observations. There is a deviation for each observation equation, and

the most probable values of the constants are determined by minimizing the sum of squares of deviations. This procedure involves taking the partial derivative of the sum with respect to each of the unknowns and setting the derivative equal to zero. This gives a number of normal equations equal to the number of unknowns. Simultaneous solution of these equations then gives the most probable values of the unknowns. The computational labor increases very rapidly, of course, as the number of unknowns increases.

2. The theory can be used when the observations are not all samples of the same parent distribution. In this case, as with one unknown, the deviations are weighted inversely as the variances of their parent distributions. For example, if the observation equations are $y_i = mx_i + b$, and the various parent distributions for the y_i are characterized by their variances σ_i^2, then the correct procedure is to minimize the quantity

$$\sum w_i d_i^2 = \sum \frac{d_i^2}{\sigma_i^2} = \sum w_i(mx_i + b - y_i)^2 \qquad (15.20)$$

where we have again used $w_i = 1/\sigma_i^2$. It is then easy to show (and is, in fact, almost obvious) that the normal equations for this example are

$$\begin{aligned}
m \sum w_i x_i + b \sum w_i &= \sum w_i y_i \\
m \sum w_i x_i^2 + b \sum w_i x_i &= \sum w_i x_i y_i
\end{aligned} \qquad (15.21)$$

As in the unweighted case, we can next calculate the variances of m and b by straightforward extensions of the methods already presented.

3. The method of least squares can be used when the observation equations are nonlinear. As a simple example, consider a capacitor of capacitance C which is initially charged to a potential V_0 and allowed to discharge through a resistance R. It can be shown that the potential difference across the capacitor is given by

$$V = V_0 e^{-t/RC} \tag{15.22}$$

Suppose we want to determine the quantity RC by making a series of observations of V at various times. Suppose further that we have very accurate time-measuring instruments, so that the only significant random errors are in V, and that we have carefully eliminated any systematic errors in these measurements.

We write an observation equation for each pair of observations:

$$V_i \overset{\circ}{=} V_0 e^{-t_i/RC} \tag{15.23}$$

and a corresponding deviation

$$d_i = V_i - V_0 e^{-t_i/RC} \tag{15.24}$$

Assuming that the errors in the V_i are normally distributed, all with the same variance, we determine V_0 and RC using the principle of maximum likelihood by computing $\Sigma\, d_i^2$ and minimizing it. The normal equations for V_0 and RC are, however, nonlinear, and can be solved only by numerical methods.

If the voltmeter happens to have a logarithmic scale, as some electronic voltmeters do, the problem becomes much simpler. We take logarithms of both sides of Eq. (15.23):

$$\ln V_i \overset{\circ}{=} \ln V_0 - \frac{t_i}{RC} \qquad (15.25)$$

Introducing a new variable y, defined by $y = \ln V$, we now have a *linear* observation equation in y_i and t_i. Furthermore, because of the logarithmic scale, it is reasonable to assume that the errors in the y_i all have the same variance; so we may proceed with exactly the same methods which led to Eqs. (15.11). If the scale is not logarithmic, the y_i will not have the same variance, however.

It is not always possible to reduce an equation to linear form by a simple substitution. In more complicated cases it may be expedient to calculate approximate values of the unknown quantities and then represent the nonlinear equations by linear approximations, using Taylor series expansions.

4. It sometimes happens that we do not know the form of the observation equations or, indeed, whether the observed quantities are related at all. We then need a systematic method of investigating whether there *is* any relationship between two variables. This leads to the theory of correlations, a simple example of which is given in Sec. 16.

16 | Correlations

In Sec. 15, we discussed the problem of determining the constants in a linear equation relating two variables (in this case x and y) by using pairs of observations (x_i, y_i)

of these variables; it was known in advance that such a linear relationship existed.

Sometimes it happens, however, that we do not know in advance whether two variables, say x and y, are related. Furthermore, if we make pairs of observations (x_i, y_i) as before, the data may be scattered so widely because of experimental errors that it is not clear whether

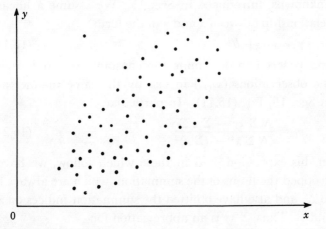

Fig. 16.1. To what extent are x and y related?

or not there is any relation between x and y. Representing the observations (x_i, y_i) graphically, we might obtain a picture similar to Fig. 16.1. Are x and y related, or are they not? Is there a *correlation* between x and y?

Of course, there is no end to the variety of possible functional relationships between x and y. There is no general way of investigating all possible relationships, but it is fairly easy to check some simple ones. The simplest possible one, of course, is a linear equation. So a reasonable place to start is to ask whether there is a *linear* relationship between x and y or, in other words, a *linear correlation*.

We can answer this question at least partially by a slight extension of the method of least squares for two unknowns, introduced in Sec. 15. We assume a linear relationship between x and y in the form

$$y = mx + b \tag{16.1}$$

and proceed to determine the constants m and b from the observations (x_i, y_i) in exactly the same manner as in Sec. 15, Eq. (15.11). In particular,

$$m = \frac{N \sum xy - \sum x \sum y}{N \sum x^2 - (\sum x)^2} \tag{16.2}$$

In this expression, and in those which follow, we have dropped the limits of the summation, which are always 1 to N, and also have omitted the summation indices on x and y. Thus, $\sum xy$ is an abbreviation for

$$\sum_{i=1}^{N} x_i y_i$$

The graphical interpretation of the procedure just described is as follows: We are trying to represent the scattered points in Fig. 16.1 by drawing the *best straight line* through the points. The slope of this line is m, and its intercept on the y axis is b. Since the deviations we have used in the method of least squares are

$$d_i = mx_i + b - y_i \tag{16.3}$$

d_i represents the vertical distance between the point (x_i, y_i) and the straight line described by constants m and b. In this case, then, the method of least squares minimizes the sum of the squares of the vertical distances between the point and the straight line. The line determined by this procedure is sometimes called the *line of regression of y on x.*

If there is no correlation at all between x and y, this sum of squares will be minimized by a horizontal line; we shall find therefore in the case of *no* correlation that $m = 0$, a line with zero slope.

Now let us back up slightly. There is no particular reason for writing our assumed linear relationship between x and y in the particular form of Eq. (16.1). We might equally well have written instead

$$x = m'y + b' \tag{16.4}$$

in which the roles of x and y have been reversed. In this case, the deviations we use in the method of least squares are given by

$$d_i' = m'y_i + b' - x_i \tag{16.5}$$

The method of least squares now minimizes the sum of the squares of the *horizontal* distances between the line described by Eq. (16.4) and the points (x_i, y_i) representing the observations. The result is the *line of regression of x on y.* The expression for m' is obtained simply by reversing the roles of x and y in Eq. (16.2) and is

$$m' = \frac{N \sum xy - \sum x \sum y}{N \sum y^2 - (\sum y)^2} \tag{16.6}$$

Note that m' is not the slope of the line given by Eq. (16.4) but rather its reciprocal. This is easy to see if we solve Eq. (16.4) for y.

$$y = \frac{x}{m'} - \frac{b'}{m'} \tag{16.7}$$

We see that the slope of this line is $1/m'$, and its intercept with the y axis is $-b'/m'$.

Using Eq. (16.4), if there is no correlation between x and y, the method of least squares will give the value $m' = 0$, a *vertical* line. If, on the other hand, all the points lie exactly on the line, so that the correlation is perfect, then this method must give us the same line as the previous one, Eq. (16.1). That is, in the case of perfect correlation, we must find that $1/m' = m$. Thus if there is *no* correlation between x and y, $mm' = 0$, while if the correlation is *perfect*, $mm' = 1$. Clearly, the value of the product mm' has something to do with the extent to which the variables x and y are correlated.

It is therefore natural to define a *correlation coefficient* r as follows:

$$r = \sqrt{mm'} = \frac{N \Sigma xy - \Sigma x \Sigma y}{[N \Sigma x^2 - (\Sigma x)^2]^{1/2} [N \Sigma y^2 - (\Sigma y)^2]^{1/2}} \tag{16.8}$$

Thus $r = 1$ means perfect correlation, and $r = 0$ means no correlation. If there is imperfect correlation, we expect a value of r somewhere between 0 and 1. In fact, it can be shown that Eq. (16.8) must *always* have a value between -1 and 1.

Suppose now that we have calculated r for a set of

observations. How do we interpret the result? In other words, how large must r be in order to indicate a significant correlation between the variables x and y? Clearly, because of random fluctuations, we will not in general get *exactly* $r = 0$ even if there is no real connection between x and y. And if a linear relationship exists, we will not get *exactly* $r = 1$, especially if the experimental errors are large. Given a value of r, then, the question to ask is: What is the probability of obtaining a value of r as large as this purely by *chance* from observations on two variables which are not really related? This situation is similar to the one which arose in interpreting the results of a χ^2 calculation in Sec. 11.

Tables have been calculated which give the probability of obtaining a given value of r for various numbers N of pairs of observations. Table V gives a few values of this probability. A reference to more extensive tables is also given.

Here is an example of the use of this table. Suppose we make 10 observations; then $N = 10$. The table says that there is a probability $P = 0.10$ of finding a correlation coefficient of 0.549 or larger by chance, and a probability $P = 0.01$ of finding $r \geq 0.765$, if the variables are not really related. If for our 10 observations we find $r = 0.9$, we can be reasonably sure that this indicates a true correlation and not an accident. But if we find only $r = 0.5$ we cannot be sure, because there is more than 10% chance that this value will occur by chance.

A commonly used rule of thumb in interpreting values of r is to regard the correlation as significant if there is less than 1 chance in 20 ($P = 0.05$) that the value will occur by chance. According to this rule of thumb, we find from Table V that for 10 sets of observations, any value of r greater than 0.632 should be regarded as showing a significant correlation. For five sets, r must be greater than 0.878 to be significant.

The theory of correlations can be extended in several directions. First, there may exist a functional relationship between x and y which is not linear and which is not detected by our linear correlation coefficient. For example, if the graph of x versus y is a circle, the correlation coefficient will be zero even if there are no experimental errors. To take such possibilities as this into account, we can assume a quadratic, cubic, or more complicated functional relationship and use the theory of least squares to determine the constants in the equations. Such an analysis gives us *nonlinear correlations*.

It is also necessary at times to consider correlations among more than two variables, so-called *multiple correlations*. These extensions of the theory of correlations have rather specialized applications, and we shall not consider them here.

PROBLEMS

1. Find the standard deviation of the mean in Prob. 18, Chap. I.

2. Find the standard deviation of the mean in Prob. 27, Chap. III. Compare this value with the *change* in the mean which results from the rejection of unlikely data.

3. A certain quantity was measured N times, and the mean and its standard deviation were computed. If it is desired to increase the precision of the result (decrease σ) by a factor of 2, how many *additional* measurements should be made?

4. In Prob. 3, discuss how the mean of the first N measurements should be combined with the mean of the additional measurements, and how the standard deviation of the result should be computed from the standard deviations of the two sets.

5. Show that the standard deviation of a weighted mean is always smaller than any individual standard deviation. Is this a reasonable result?

6. Two different measurements of the speed of light using the same general method (a rotating mirror) yielded the following results:

299,796 ± 4 km/sec
299,774 ± 2 km/sec

Are these results consistent? (Assume that the errors given are standard deviations of the means.)

7. In Prob. 13, Chap. I, suppose that the "errors" referred to are standard deviations of the means. Find the standard deviation in g. Compare with the result of Prob. 13, Chap. I. Which is more significant?

8. For some obscure reason an individual wants to make an accurate determination of the area of a sheet of typewriting paper. The following measurements are made on the length and width:

Length, in.	Width, in.
11.03	8.51
11.00	8.48
10.97	8.49
10.98	8.50
11.02	8.53
	8.48
	8.51

a. Determine the standard deviation of each set of measurements.

b. Determine the most probable value of each quantity and its standard deviation.

c. Determine the most probable value of the area and its standard deviation.

9. In a centripetal-force experiment the force exerted on a body moving in a circle with constant speed is measured directly and is also computed from the equation

$$F = \frac{mv^2}{R} = \frac{4\pi^2 mR}{T^2}$$

The following data were obtained:

F, dynes	T, sec	R, cm
6.92×10^5	0.200	5.13
6.82	0.198	5.06
6.87	0.202	5.05
6.87	0.199	5.09
6.92	0.201	5.10

The mass is known very accurately: $m = 140.00$ g. Do the measured and calculated values of F agree? Discuss.

10. In the Bohr theory of the structure of the hydrogen atom, the energies of the various quantum states are given by

$$E_n = -\frac{1}{2}\frac{me^4}{n^2\hbar^2}$$

where m is the mass of the electron, e is its charge, $\hbar$ is Planck's constant divided by 2π, and $n = 1, 2, 3, \cdots$. If the mass is known with a fractional standard deviation of 0.1%, the charge with 0.2%, and Planck's constant with 0.1%, what is the per cent standard deviation in E_n for the state for which $n = 1$? For the $n = 2$ state? If the accuracy is to be improved, which quantity (m, e, or $\hbar$) should be determined more accurately?

11. The phase angle ϕ between voltage V and current I supplied to an electric motor (or any other device) is related to the electrical power input P by the equation $P = EI \cos \phi$. The quantities P, E, and I are measured, with the following results:

$P = 515 \pm 50$ watts
$E = 110 \pm 2$ volts
$I = 5.20 \pm 0.20$ amp

a. The quantity $\cos \phi$ is called the *power factor*. Calculate the power factor and its standard deviation.

b. Calculate ϕ and its standard deviation.

12. The number of radioactive decays occurring in a given interval has been shown to follow the Poisson distribution. Often the parameter a is not known in advance, but is determined by counting for several intervals. Suppose N intervals are used, and n_i counts are observed in interval i (where $i = 1, 2, \cdots, N$). Apply the principle of maximum likelihood to determine a. That is, find the value of a which maximizes the probability of occurrence of the set of observa-

tions n_i. Specifically, show directly that the most probable value of a is the *average* of the n_i.

13. What is the standard deviation of the most probable value of a obtained in Prob. 12?

14. The value of a resistor R is to be found by passing several different currents I through it, measuring the corresponding voltage drop V, and using the relation $V = IR$. The values of V are measured very precisely with a potentiometer, while I is measured with an ordinary ammeter, resulting in normally distributed random errors. Using the method of least squares, derive an expression for the most probable value of R in terms of the pairs of observations (V_i, I_i).

15. From the set of observation equations given, find the most probable values of x and y, using the method of least squares, assuming all the observational errors to belong to the same normal distribution.

$$3x + y \overset{\circ}{=} 2.9$$
$$x - 2y \overset{\circ}{=} 0.9$$
$$2x - 3y \overset{\circ}{=} 1.9$$

16. The three interior angles of a triangle were observed to be

$$31° \qquad 62° \qquad 88°$$

Using the method of least squares and the fact that the sum of the angles must be 180°, find the most probable values of the angles. Does your method make any assumption about relative accuracies of the measurements of the angles?

17. In an experiment to measure the acceleration of a freely falling object, a tuning fork is set into vibration and allowed to drop, scratching a wavy line on a strip of waxed paper as it falls. From this trace, the positions at a succession

of times separated by equal time intervals can be determined. The theoretical relation between distance and time is

$$s = s_0 + v_0 t + \tfrac{1}{2}gt^2$$

Assuming that the times are known much more precisely than the positions, use the method of least squares to derive expressions for the initial position s_0, the initial velocity v_0, and the acceleration g in terms of the pairs of observations (s_i, t_i).

18. Use the method of least squares to find the best straight line for the four points (4,5), (6,8), (8,10), (9,12). Are any assumptions regarding the errors necessary?

19. An experimenter wanted to determine the ratio of inches to centimeters by using a yardstick and a meter stick, side by side. His procedure is to observe the centimeter corresponding to each a succession of inch marks. Unfortunately, the centimeters are not subdivided, so he reads only to the nearest centimeter. Use the method of least squares to derive a formula for the conversion factor.

20. In Prob. 19, the result is considerably simpler if an odd number of inch marks are used, and if they are renumbered so that zero is in the middle. That is, if there are $2N + 1$ marks, they are labeled from $-N$ to N. Obtain the simplified result, using this scheme. Useful information: The sum of the first N integers is

$$1 + 2 + \cdots + N = \frac{N(N + 1)}{2}$$

and the sum of their squares is

$$1^2 + 2^2 + \cdots + N^2 = \frac{N(N + 1)(2N + 1)}{6}$$

21. Using the data of Prob. 18, calculate the line of regres-

sion of x on y, the line of regression of y on x, and the correlation coefficient. Is the correlation significant?

22. Following are two sets of pairs of observations on variables x and y:

x	y	x	y
1	2	1	2
2	3	2	3
3	3	3	4
4	2	4	5
5	4	5	5

Determine whether either of these sets exhibits a significant correlation between x and y.

APPENDIX A
SUMMARY OF FORMULAS

Following is a summary of important and useful formulas which have been developed in the text. The numbered equations are given the same numbers as in the text to facilitate reference to appropriate parts of the text.

Approximations

If a quantity Q is determined from quantities a, b, . . . by a relation $Q = f(a, b, \ldots)$, then the change ΔQ of the quantity produced by changes Δa, Δb, . . . is

$$\Delta Q = \frac{\partial Q}{\partial a} \Delta a + \frac{\partial Q}{\partial b} \Delta b + \frac{\partial Q}{\partial c} \Delta c + \cdots \qquad (2.8)$$

The Mean and Dispersion

The *mean* (or arithmetic mean or average) of a set of N numbers, of which a typical one is x_i, is

$$\bar{x} = \frac{1}{N} \sum_{i=1}^{N} x_i \qquad (3.2)$$

The *weighted mean* of a set of N numbers, of which a typical one is x_i with weight w_i, is

$$\bar{x} = \frac{w_1x_1 + w_2x_2 + \cdots + w_Nx_N}{w_1 + w_2 + \cdots + w_N} = \frac{\displaystyle\sum_{i=1}^{N} w_ix_i}{\displaystyle\sum_{i=1}^{N} w_i} \qquad (3.3)$$

The *deviation* of a number x_i in a set of N numbers is

$$d_i = x_i - \bar{x} \qquad (3.4)$$

The *mean deviation* of a set of N numbers x_i is

$$\alpha = \frac{1}{N} \sum_{i=1}^{N} |d_i| = \frac{1}{N} \sum_{i=1}^{N} |x_i - \bar{x}| \qquad (3.8)$$

The *standard deviation* of a set of N numbers x_i is

$$\sigma = \sqrt{\frac{1}{N} \sum_{i=1}^{N} d_i^2} = \sqrt{\frac{1}{N} \sum_{i=1}^{N} (x_i - \bar{x})^2} \qquad (3.9)$$

The *variance* is defined as the square of the *standard deviation*.

Probability

If the probabilities for two independent events a and b are P_a and P_b, the probability for *both* to occur is the product P_aP_b. If events a and b are mutually exclusive, the probability for a *or* b to occur is the sum $P_a + P_b$.

Permutations and Combinations

The number of permutations of N objects is

$$N! = N(N - 1)(N - 2)(N - 3) \cdots (4)(3)(2)(1) \qquad (5.1)$$

The number of combinations of N objects, taken n at a time, is

$$C(N,n) = \frac{N!}{(N - n)!\, n!} = \binom{N}{n} \tag{5.3}$$

which also defines the binomial coefficients.

The *binomial theorem* for expansion of the binomial $(a + b)^N$ is

$$(a + b)^N = \sum_{n=0}^{N} \binom{N}{n} a^{N-n}b^n$$

$$= \sum_{n=0}^{N} \frac{N!}{(N - n)!\, n!} a^{N-n}b^n \tag{5.6}$$

The sum of the binomial coefficients for a given N is

$$(1 + 1)^N = 2^N = \sum_{n=0}^{N} \binom{N}{n} \tag{5.7}$$

Probability Distributions

The condition for a discrete probability distribution to be *normalized* is

$$\sum_{n} f(n) = 1 \tag{6.1}$$

The *mean* of a discrete probability distribution is

$$\bar{n} = \sum_{n} n f(n) \tag{6.2}$$

The *variance* of a discrete probability distribution is

$$\sigma^2 = \sum_{n} (n - \bar{n})^2 f(n) \tag{6.4}$$

The best estimate of the variance of a parent distribution, from a sample of this distribution, is

$$\sigma = \sqrt{\frac{1}{N-1} \sum_{i=1}^{N} (x_i - \bar{x})^2} \tag{6.5}$$

Binomial Distribution

The *binomial distribution* gives the probability of n successes in N independent trials, if the probability of success in any one trial is p. The binomial distribution is given by

$$f_{N,p}(n) = \binom{N}{n} p^n q^{N-n} \tag{7.1}$$

where $q = 1 - p$.

The *mean* of the binomial distribution is

$$\bar{n} = \sum_{n=0}^{N} n \binom{N}{n} p^n (1-p)^{N-n} = Np \tag{7.5}$$

The *variance* of the binomial distribution is

$$\sigma^2 = Np(1-p) = Npq \tag{7.7}$$

Poisson Distribution

The *Poisson distribution* is the limit of the binomial distribution as $N \to \infty$ and $p \to 0$ in such a way that the product $a = Np$ remains finite. The Poisson distribution is given by

$$f_a(n) = \frac{a^n e^{-a}}{n!} \tag{8.5}$$

The *mean* of the Poisson distribution is

$$\bar{n} = a \tag{8.6}$$

The *variance* of the Poisson distribution is

$$\sigma^2 = a. \tag{8.9}$$

Gauss Distribution

The *Gauss distribution*, or *normal error function*, is

$$f(x) = \frac{h}{\sqrt{\pi}} e^{-h^2(x-m)^2} = \frac{1}{\sqrt{2\pi}\,\sigma} e^{-(x-m)^2/2\sigma^2} \tag{9.9, 9.16}$$

The *index of precision* h and the *variance* σ^2 are related by

$$\sigma^2 = \frac{1}{2h^2} \tag{9.15}$$

The *mean deviation* for the Gauss distribution is given by

$$\alpha = \frac{1}{\sqrt{\pi}\,h} = \sqrt{\frac{2}{\pi}}\,\sigma \tag{9.18, 9.19}$$

The probability for a measurement to fall within $T\sigma$ of the mean is

$$P(T) = \frac{1}{\sqrt{2\pi}} \int_{-T}^{T} e^{-t^2/2}\,dt \tag{9.22}$$

The Gauss distribution is approximately equal to the binomial distribution with the same mean and variance, if N is very large and p is finite. For very large N,

$$f_{N,p}(n) = \frac{N!}{(N-n)!\,n!}\,p^n q^{N-n}$$

$$\cong \frac{1}{\sqrt{2\pi Npq}}\,e^{-(n-Np)^2/2Npq} \tag{C.25}$$

Appendix A

Goodness of Fit

To compare a sample frequency $F(n)$ with a frequency $Nf(n)$ predicted by a parent distribution $f(n)$ for N trials, a suitable index of goodness of fit is

$$\chi^2 = \sum_n \frac{[Nf(n) - F(n)]^2}{Nf(n)} \tag{11.1}$$

In using a table of values of χ^2, $\nu = K - r$, where K is the number of frequencies of the two distributions compared and r is the number of parameters of the parent distribution which are determined from the sample.

Standard Deviation of the Mean

The *standard deviation of the mean* $\bar{x}$ of a set of numbers x_i is

$$\sigma_m{}^2 = \frac{\sigma^2}{N} \qquad \text{or} \qquad \sigma_m = \frac{\sigma}{\sqrt{N}} \tag{12.6}$$

if the numbers are distributed normally with parent standard deviation σ.

Propagation of Errors

If a quantity Q is determined from quantities $a, b, \ldots$ by a relation $Q = f(a, b, \ldots)$, the variance of the mean of Q is related to the variances of the means of $a, b, \ldots$ by

$$\sigma_{mQ}{}^2 = \left(\frac{\partial Q}{\partial a}\right)^2 \sigma_{ma}{}^2 + \left(\frac{\partial Q}{\partial b}\right)^2 \sigma_{mb}{}^2 + \cdots \tag{13.8}$$

Method of Least Squares

If N observations are made on a quantity, and their errors are normally distributed, the *most probable value* of the quantity is

$$x = \frac{1}{N} \sum_{i=1}^{N} x_i \qquad (14.4)$$

and the *variance* of the most probable value is related to the variance of the individual observations by

$$\sigma_m^2 = \sum \frac{\sigma^2}{N^2} = \frac{\sigma^2}{N} \qquad (14.10)$$

If the observations x_i come from different parent distributions, characterized by their variances σ_i^2, then the most probable value of x is the weighted mean

$$x = \frac{\sum x_i/\sigma_i^2}{\sum 1/\sigma_i^2} \qquad (14.13)$$

and the *variance* of this weighted mean is given by

$$\frac{1}{\sigma_m^2} = \sum_i \frac{1}{\sigma_i^2} \qquad (14.16)$$

In an equation $y = mx + b$, the *most probable values* of m and b, from a set of pairs of observations (x_i, y_i) in which the x_i have no errors and all the y_i have errors belonging to the same distribution, are

$$m = \frac{N \sum x_i y_i - (\sum x_i)(\sum y_i)}{N \sum x_i^2 - (\sum x_i)^2}$$

$$b = \frac{(\sum y_i)(\sum x_i^2) - (\sum x_i y_i)(\sum x_i)}{N \sum x_i^2 - (\sum x_i)^2} \qquad (15.11)$$

The *variances* of the most probable values are given by

$$\sigma_m{}^2 = \frac{N\sigma^2}{\Delta} \tag{15.16}$$

and

$$\sigma_b{}^2 = \frac{\sigma^2 \Sigma x_i{}^2}{\Delta} \tag{15.17}$$

where

$$\Delta = N \Sigma x_i{}^2 - (\Sigma x_i)^2$$

and

$$\sigma^2 = \frac{1}{N} \Sigma (mx_i + b - y_i)^2 \tag{15.19}$$

where σ^2 is evaluated using the most probable values of m and b.

Correlations

The definition of the *linear correlation coefficient r* is

$$r = \sqrt{mm'} = \frac{N \Sigma xy - \Sigma x \Sigma y}{[N \Sigma x^2 - (\Sigma x)^2]^{1/2} [N \Sigma y^2 - (\Sigma y)^2]^{1/2}} \tag{16.8}$$

APPENDIX B

EVALUATION OF $\bar{n}$ AND σ FOR BINOMIAL DISTRIBUTION

To evaluate the sum

$$\bar{n} = \sum_{n=0}^{N} n \binom{N}{n} p^n (1-p)^{N-n} \tag{B.1}$$

we note that it is similar to an expression we have already encountered in considering the *normalization* of the binomial distribution, namely,

$$\sum_{n=0}^{N} \binom{N}{n} p^n (1-p)^{N-n} = 1 \tag{B.2}$$

The difference is that the sum in Eq. (B.1) contains an extra factor of n. But by means of a trick we can convert this into the form of the sum in Eq. (B.2).

From here on we drop the limits on the sums, as we did in Sec. 3, remembering always that n ranges from 0 to N. Now we differentiate both sides of Eq. (B.2) with respect to p, which is legitimate because the equation is true for all values of p between 0 and 1, as observed earlier. The advantage of doing this will appear shortly. Taking the derivative,

$$\sum \binom{N}{n} [np^{n-1}(1-p)^{N-n} - (N-n)p^n(1-p)^{N-n-1}]$$

$$= 0 \quad \text{(B.3)}$$

This can be rewritten

$$\sum \binom{N}{n} np^{n-1}(1-p)^{N-n}$$

$$= \sum \binom{N}{n}(N-n)p^n(1-p)^{N-n-1}$$

$$= N \sum \binom{N}{n}p^n(1-p)^{N-n-1}$$

$$- \sum \binom{N}{n} np^n(1-p)^{N-n-1}$$

or

$$\sum n \binom{N}{n}[p^{n-1}(1-p)^{N-n} + p^n(1-p)^{N-n-1}]$$

$$= N \sum \binom{N}{n}p^n(1-p)^{N-n-1} \quad \text{(B.4)}$$

We now multiply both sides of the equation by $p(1-p)$:

$$\sum n \binom{N}{n}[(1-p)p^n(1-p)^{N-n} + pp^n(1-p)^{N-n}]$$

$$= Np \sum \binom{N}{n}p^n(1-p)^{N-n} \quad \text{(B.5)}$$

Combining the two terms on the left side, and using Eq. (B.2) in the right side

$$\sum n \binom{N}{n}p^n(1-p)^{N-n} = \sum n f_{N,p}(n) = Np \quad \text{(B.6)}$$

Now the left side of this expression is just our original expression for $\bar{n}$, Eq. (B.1); hence we conclude that

$$\bar{n} = Np \qquad \text{(B.7)}$$

The calculation of σ^2 proceeds in a similar manner. The variance is given by Eq. (7.6), which we give again for convenience:

$$\sigma^2 = \Sigma \, (n - Np)^2 f_{N,p}(n) \tag{B.8}$$

To evaluate this sum we first rewrite Eq. (B.8) as

$$\sigma^2 = \Sigma \, (n^2 - 2nNp + N^2p^2) f_{N,p}(n)$$
$$= \Sigma \, n^2 f_N(n) - 2Np \, \Sigma \, n f_{N,p}(n) + N^2 p^2 \, \Sigma \, f_{N,p}(n) \tag{B.9}$$

The sums in the second and third terms are already known from Eqs. (B.6) and (B.2), respectively; using these, we find

$$\sigma^2 = \Sigma \, n^2 f_{N,p}(n) - (Np)^2 \tag{B.10}$$

To evaluate $\Sigma \, n^2 f_{N,p}(n)$ we differentiate Eq. (B.6):

$$\sum n \binom{N}{n} [n p^{n-1}(1 - p)^{N-n}$$
$$- (N - n)p^n(1 - p)^{N-n-1}] = N \tag{B.11}$$

We multiply by $p(1 - p)$ and rearrange terms as before, to obtain

$$\sum n^2 \binom{N}{n} p^n(1 - p)^{N-n}$$
$$- Np \sum n \binom{N}{n} p^n(1 - p)^{N-n} = Np(1 - p) \tag{B.12}$$

Finally, using Eq. (B.6) again,

$$\sum n^2 \binom{N}{n} p^n (1-p)^{N-n} = (Np)^2 + Np(1-p)$$

$$(B.13)$$

or

$$\Sigma\, n^2 f_N(n) = Np(1 - p + Np) \qquad\qquad (B.14)$$

Now, inserting this result into Eq. (B.10), we obtain

$$\sigma^2 = Np(1 - p + Np) - (Np)^2 = Np(1-p) = Npq$$

$$(B.15)$$

or

$$\sigma = \sqrt{Npq} \qquad\qquad (B.16)$$

as stated in Sec. 7.

APPENDIX C

DERIVATION OF GAUSS DISTRIBUTION

Following is a derivation of the Gauss distribution function from some plausible assumptions. It is not intended as a substitute for empirical verification of this distribution, but as evidence that it *can* be derived from basic considerations. To be honest we must state that the mathematical derivation can be simplified considerably by making use of an approximation formula for factorials of large numbers (Stirling's formula). The use of this formula has been avoided here because, to a reader who is not familiar with its derivation, the development of the Gauss distribution using it is not likely to be very convincing.

We begin by assuming that the random error in a measurement is composed of a large number N of elementary errors, all of equal magnitude ϵ, and each equally likely to be positive or negative. With these assumptions, we can calculate the probability of occurrence of any particular error in the range $(-N\epsilon)$ to $(+N\epsilon)$. Having done this, we take the limit of this distribution as the number N becomes infinitely large and the magnitude ϵ infinitesimally small in such a way that the *standard deviation* of the distribution remains constant.

First, we note that the probability for n of the elementary errors to be positive and the other $N - n$ to be negative is given by the binomial distribution with $p = q = \frac{1}{2}$. The corresponding error, which we shall call y, is given by

$$y = n\epsilon - (N - n)\epsilon = (2n - N)\epsilon \qquad \text{(C.1)}$$

The probability of occurrence of this particular error is

$$f_{N,1/2}(n) = \frac{N!}{(N - n)!\, n!\, 2^N} \qquad \text{(C.2)}$$

For future reference, we compute the standard deviation of y. Because each elementary error is as likely to be positive as negative, the mean value of y is zero. Therefore the standard deviation is given simply by

$$\sigma^2 = \Sigma\, y^2 f_{N,1/2}(n) = \Sigma\, (2n - N)^2\epsilon^2 f_{N,1/2}(n) \qquad \text{(C.3)}$$

This sum is easily evaluated with the help of Eqs. (B.1), (B.2), and (B.14), setting $p = \frac{1}{2}$ in all these:

$$\sigma^2 = 4\epsilon^2 \Sigma\, n^2 f_N(n) - 4N\epsilon^2 \Sigma\, n f_N(n) + N^2\epsilon^2 \Sigma\, f_N(n)$$

$$= 4\epsilon^2 \frac{N}{2}\left(1 - \frac{1}{2} + \frac{N}{2}\right) - 4N\epsilon^2 \frac{N}{2} + N^2\epsilon^2$$

$$= \epsilon^2 N \qquad \text{(C.4)}$$

$$\sigma = \epsilon\sqrt{N} \qquad \text{(C.5)}$$

To simplify notation in the following developments, we introduce a new index r, defined by the equation

$$2r = 2n - N \qquad \text{(C.6)}$$

One immediate advantage of this change is suggested by Eq. (C.1), which now becomes simply

$$y = 2r\epsilon \qquad \text{(C.7)}$$

Note that since the range of n is 0 to N, the range of r is from $-N/2$ to $+N/2$, in steps of unity. Furthermore, if N is *even*, r is always an *integer*, while if N is *odd*, r is always a *half-integer*. In either case, the quantities $N/2 + r$ and $N/2 - r$ which appear below are always integers.

We now express the probability for the error $y = 2r\epsilon$ in terms of the index r, using Eq. (C.6) in the form $n = r + N/2$. Equation (C.2) then becomes

$$f_{N,1/2}(r) = \frac{N!}{\left(\dfrac{N}{2} - r\right)! \left(\dfrac{N}{2} + r\right)! \, 2^N} \tag{C.8}$$

The next larger possible value of the error y results from replacing r in Eq. (C.7) by $(r + 1)$. This error is then larger by an amount 2ϵ; so we call it $y + 2\epsilon$. The corresponding probability is obtained by inserting $(r + 1)$ for r in Eq. (3.8):

$$f_{N,1/2}(r + 1) = \frac{N!}{\left(\dfrac{N}{2} - r - 1\right)! \left(\dfrac{N}{2} + r + 1\right)! \, 2^N} \tag{C.9}$$

Thus if we call $f(y)$ the probability of occurrence of error y, we have

$$f(y) = \frac{N!}{\left(\dfrac{N}{2} - r\right)! \left(\dfrac{N}{2} + r\right)! \, 2^N} \tag{C.10}$$

$$f(y + 2\epsilon) = \frac{N!}{\left(\dfrac{N}{2} - r - 1\right)! \left(\dfrac{N}{2} + r + 1\right)! \, 2^N}$$

These expressions are both rather complicated, but we note immediately that their *quotient* is fairly simple. That is,

$$\frac{f(y + 2\epsilon)}{f(y)} = \frac{(N/2 - r)!}{(N/2 - r - 1)!} \frac{(N/2 + r)!}{(N/2 + r + 1)!}$$

$$= \frac{N/2 - r}{N/2 + r + 1} \tag{C.11}$$

Next it is necessary to perform a somewhat tricky maneuver. Keeping in mind that we are eventually going to let $N \to \infty$ and $\epsilon \to 0$ at the same time, in such a way that the product $\sigma^2 = \epsilon^2 N$ remains constant, we now regard y as a continuous variable and $f(y)$ as a function of this variable. Because ϵ is small, we can approximate $f(y + 2\epsilon)$ as follows:

$$f(y + 2\epsilon) \cong f(y) + 2\epsilon \frac{d}{dy} f(y) \tag{C.12}$$

Also, to facilitate taking the limit, it is convenient to express r and ϵ in terms of y, N, and σ, using Eqs. (C.5) and (C.7) as follows:

$$r = \frac{y}{2\epsilon} = \frac{y\sqrt{N}}{2\sigma} \qquad \epsilon = \frac{\sigma}{\sqrt{N}} \tag{C.13}$$

Inserting Eqs. (C.12) and (C.13) into Eq. (C.11),

$$\frac{f(y) + (2\sigma/\sqrt{N})f'(y)}{f(y)} = \frac{N/2 - y\sqrt{N}/2\sigma}{N/2 + y\sqrt{N}/2\sigma + 1} \tag{C.14}$$

where we have introduced the abbreviation $f' = df/dy$. Rearranging,

$$\frac{2\sigma}{\sqrt{N}} \frac{f'(y)}{f(y)} = \frac{N/2 - y\sqrt{N}/2\sigma}{N/2 + y\sqrt{N}/2\sigma + 1} - 1 \qquad (\text{C.15})$$

and

$$\frac{f'(y)}{f(y)} = -\frac{y/\sigma^2 + 1/\sqrt{N}\sigma}{1 + (y/\sqrt{N}\sigma + 2/N)} \qquad (\text{C.16})$$

Now, at last, we are ready to consider the limit of Eq. (C.16) as $N \to \infty$ while σ is constant. Clearly, in both numerator and denominator, the second term becomes very small compared to the first, if N is sufficiently large. So in the limit the terms containing $1/\sqrt{N}$ and $1/N$ both vanish, and we have simply

$$\frac{f'(y)}{f(y)} = -\frac{y}{\sigma^2} \qquad (\text{C.17})$$

This is a differential equation for the desired function $f(y)$; it is easily solved by noting that

$$\frac{f'(y)}{f(y)} = \frac{d}{dy} \ln f(y)$$

Making this substitution and integrating both sides of the equation, we find

$$\ln f(y) = -\frac{y^2}{2\sigma^2} + \text{const} \qquad (\text{C.18})$$

We represent the integration constant by $\ln A$, where A is another constant, and take antilogs of both sides, to obtain

$$f(y) = Ae^{-y^2/2\sigma^2} \qquad (\text{C.19})$$

The value of the constant A is determined by recalling the interpretation of $f(y)$ discussed in Sec. 9. The quantity $f(y)\,dy$ is the probability that a single error will fall in the range y to $y + dy$. Since the total probability for the error to fall *somewhere* in the range of values of y (which is now, strictly speaking, $-\infty$ to $+\infty$) is unity, we must insist that

$$\int_{-\infty}^{\infty} Ae^{-y^2/2\sigma^2} = 1$$

or

$$A = \frac{1}{\int_{-\infty}^{\infty} e^{-y^2/2\sigma^2}} \tag{C.20}$$

Making the substitution $z = y/\sqrt{2}\sigma$, we obtain

$$A^{-1} = \sqrt{2}\sigma \int_{-\infty}^{\infty} e^{-z^2}\,dz \tag{C.21}$$

The integral in this expression is evaluated in Appendix D and has the value $\sqrt{\pi}$. Hence

$$A = \frac{1}{\sqrt{2\pi}\sigma} \tag{C.22}$$

and

$$f(y) = \frac{1}{\sqrt{2\pi}\sigma} e^{-y^2/2\sigma^2} \tag{C.23}$$

Finally, we express the function in terms of the *observations* rather than their errors. If y is the error corresponding to an observation x, and the true value of the observed quantity is m, then $y = x - m$. In terms of x,

$$f(x) = \frac{1}{\sqrt{2\pi}\sigma} e^{-(x-m)^2/2\sigma^2} \tag{C.24}$$

This form is usually called the Gauss distribution, or normal error function.

In the preceding discussion, the Gauss distribution has been shown to be an approximation of a distribution closely related to the binomial distribution, valid when the number N of independent events becomes very large. By similar methods it can be shown that *any* binomial distribution approaches the Gaussian form if N is very large and p is finite. Thus for large N we can represent a binomial distribution (which is very unwieldy for large N) by a Gauss distribution with the same mean and standard deviation as the binomial, namely, $m = Np$ and $\sigma = (Npq)^{1/2}$, respectively. Thus for large N we have approximately

$$f_{N,p}(n) = \frac{N!}{(N-n)!\,n!}\, p^n q^{N-n}$$

$$\cong \frac{1}{\sqrt{2\pi Npq}}\, e^{-(n-Np)^2/2Npq} \qquad \text{(C.25)}$$

It should be noted that this is *not* a suitable approximation if p is extremely small. If p grows small as N grows large, then the appropriate approximations lead instead to the Poisson distribution, discussed in Sec. 8.

APPENDIX D

EVALUATION OF NORMAL ERROR INTEGRAL

In developing the Gauss distribution, it is necessary to know the value of the integral

$$I = \int_{-\infty}^{\infty} e^{-x^2} \, dx$$

We denote the value of the integral by I. Then, since the variable of integration has no effect on the value of the result, we write

$$I^2 = \int_{-\infty}^{\infty} e^{-x^2} \, dx \int_{-\infty}^{\infty} e^{-y^2} \, dy \qquad \text{(D.1)}$$

Now Eq. (D.1) can also be interpreted as the double integral over the $x - y$ plane of the function

$$e^{-x^2} e^{-y^2} = e^{-(x^2+y^2)}$$

That is,

$$I^2 = \int_{-\infty}^{\infty} \int_{-\infty}^{\infty} e^{-(x^2+y^2)} \, dx \, dy \qquad \text{(D.2)}$$

It may help to interpret this integral geometrically. Think of a tent whose floor is the $x - y$ plane and whose height above the $x - y$ plane at any point (x, y) is

$$e^{-(x^2+y^2)}$$

Then the integrand

$$e^{-(x^2+y^2)} \, dx \, dy$$

represents the volume of a column above the element of

floor area $dx\, dy$. Thus the quantity I^2 is just the total volume enclosed by the tent and its floor.

Now we transform Eq. (D.2) into polar coordinates, using as the element of floor area $dr\, (r\, d\theta)$ instead of $dx\, dy$, and using $r^2 = x^2 + y^2$. We thus obtain

$$I^2 = \int_{r=0}^{r=\infty} \int_{\theta=0}^{\theta=2\pi} e^{-r^2} r\, dr\, d\theta \tag{D.3}$$

This integral now can be expressed in terms of two integrals, each of which contains only one of the variables, as follows:

$$I^2 = \int_0^\infty e^{-r^2} r\, dr \left[\int_0^{2\pi} d\theta \right] \tag{D.4}$$

The integration on θ is trivial and gives simply a factor 2π. The r integral can be evaluated by making the substitution $r^2 = u$.

$$I^2 = 2\pi \int_0^\infty e^{-u} \tfrac{1}{2}\, du = \pi \tag{D.5}$$

Thus

$$I = \int_{-\infty}^\infty e^{-x^2}\, dx = \sqrt{\pi} \tag{D.6}$$

Table I.   Values of the Gauss Function*

Values of the function $\dfrac{1}{\sqrt{2\pi}}\, e^{-t^2/2}$ are given for various values of t.

Each figure in the body of the table is preceded by a decimal point.

t	0.00	0.01	0.02	0.03	0.04	0.05	0.06	0.07	0.08	0.09
0.0	39894	39892	39886	39876	39862	39844	39822	39797	39767	39733
0.1	39695	39654	39608	39559	39505	39448	39387	39322	39253	39181
0.2	39104	39024	38940	38853	38762	38667	38568	38466	38361	38251
0.3	38139	38023	37903	37780	37654	37524	37391	37255	37115	36973
0.4	36827	36678	36526	36371	36213	36053	35889	35723	35553	35381
0.5	35207	35029	34849	34667	34482	34294	34105	33912	33718	33521
0.6	33322	33121	32918	32713	32506	32297	32086	31874	31659	31443
0.7	31225	31006	30785	30563	30339	30114	29887	29658	29430	29200
0.8	28969	28737	28504	28269	28034	27798	27562	27324	27086	26848
0.9	26609	26369	26129	25888	25647	25406	25164	24923	24681	24439
1.0	24197	23955	23713	23471	23230	22988	22747	22506	22265	22025
1.1	21785	21546	21307	21069	20831	20594	20357	20121	19886	19652
1.2	19419	19186	18954	18724	18494	18265	18037	17810	17585	17360
1.3	17137	16915	16694	16474	16256	16038	15822	15608	15395	15183
1.4	14973	14764	14556	14350	14146	13943	13742	13542	13344	13147
1.5	12952	12758	12566	12376	12188	12001	11816	11632	11450	11270
1.6	11092	10915	10741	10567	10396	10226	10059	09893	09728	09566
1.7	09405	09246	09089	08933	08780	08628	08478	08329	08183	08038
1.8	07895	07754	07614	07477	07341	07206	07074	06943	06814	06687
1.9	06562	06438	06316	06195	06077	05959	05844	05730	05618	05508
2.0	05399	05292	05186	05082	04980	04879	04780	04682	04586	04491
2.1	04398	04307	04217	04128	04041	03955	03871	03788	03706	03626
2.2	03547	03470	03394	03319	03246	03174	03103	03034	02965	02898
2.3	02833	02768	02705	02643	02582	02522	02463	02406	02349	02294
2.4	02239	02186	02134	02083	02033	01984	01936	01888	01842	01797
2.5	01753	01709	01667	01625	01585	01545	01506	01468	01431	01394
2.6	01358	01323	01289	01256	01223	01191	01160	01130	01100	01071
2.7	01042	01014	00987	00961	00935	00909	00885	00861	00837	00814
2.8	00792	00770	00748	00727	00707	00687	00668	00649	00631	00613
2.9	00595	00578	00562	00545	00530	00514	00499	00485	00470	00457
3.0	00443									
3.5	008727									
4.0	0001338									
4.5	0000160									
5.0	000001487									

* This table was adapted, by permission, from F. C. Kent, "Elements of Statistics," McGraw-Hill Book Company, Inc., New York, 1924.
A more complete table is "Tables of Normal Probability Functions," National Bureau of Standards, Washington, 1953.

Table II. Integrals of the Gauss Function*

Values of the integral $\dfrac{1}{\sqrt{2\pi}} \displaystyle\int_0^T e^{-t^2/2}\, dt$ are given for various values of T. To evaluate Eq. (9.22) in the text, use the relation

$$\frac{1}{\sqrt{2\pi}} \int_{-T}^T e^{-t^2/2}\, dt = 2\,\frac{1}{\sqrt{2\pi}} \int_0^T e^{-t^2/2}\, dt$$

A related function which is sometimes used is erf z, defined by

$$\text{erf } z = \frac{1}{\sqrt{\pi}} \int_{-z}^z e^{-x^2}\, dx$$

The values given here are equal to $\tfrac{1}{2}$ erf $(T/\sqrt{2})$.
Each figure in the body of the table is preceded by a decimal point.

T	0.00	0.01	0.02	0.03	0.04	0.05	0.06	0.07	0.08	0.09
0.0	00000	00399	00798	01197	01595	01994	02392	02790	03188	03586
0.1	03983	04380	04776	05172	05567	05962	06356	06749	07142	07535
0.2	07926	08317	08706	09095	09483	09871	10257	10642	11026	11409
0.3	11791	12172	12552	12930	13307	13683	14058	14431	14803	15173
0.4	15554	15910	16276	16640	17003	17364	17724	18082	18439	18793
0.5	19146	19497	19847	20194	20450	20884	21226	21566	21904	22240
0.6	22575	22907	23237	23565	23891	24215	24537	24857	25175	25490
0.7	25804	26115	26424	26730	27035	27337	27637	27935	28230	28524
0.8	28814	29103	29389	29673	29955	30234	30511	30785	31057	31327
0.9	31594	31859	32121	32381	32639	32894	33147	33398	33646	33891
1.0	34134	34375	34614	34850	35083	35313	35543	35769	35993	36214
1.1	36433	36650	36864	37076	37286	37493	37698	37900	38100	38298
1.2	38493	38686	38877	39065	39251	39435	39617	39796	39973	40147
1.3	40320	40490	40658	40824	40988	41149	41308	41466	41621	41774
1.4	41924	42073	42220	42364	42507	42647	42786	42922	43056	43189
1.5	43319	43448	43574	43699	43822	43943	44062	44179	44295	44408
1.6	44520	44630	44738	44845	44950	45053	45154	45254	45352	45449
1.7	45543	45637	45728	45818	45907	45994	46080	46164	46246	46327
1.8	46407	46485	46562	46638	46712	46784	46856	46926	46995	47062
1.9	47128	47193	47257	47320	47381	47441	47500	47558	47615	47670
2.0	47725	47778	47831	47882	47932	47982	48030	48077	48124	48169
2.1	48214	48257	48300	48341	48382	48422	48461	48500	48537	48574
2.2	48610	48645	48679	48713	48745	48778	48809	48840	48870	48899
2.3	48928	48956	48983	49010	49036	49061	49086	49111	49134	49158
2.4	49180	49202	49224	49245	49266	49286	49305	49324	49343	49361
2.5	49379	49396	49413	49430	49446	49461	49477	49492	49506	49520
2.6	49534	49547	49560	49573	49585	49598	49609	49621	49632	49643
2.7	49653	49664	49674	49683	49693	49702	49711	49720	49728	49736
2.8	49744	49752	49760	49767	49774	49781	49788	49795	49801	49807
2.9	49813	49819	49825	49831	49836	49841	49846	49851	49856	49861
3.0	49865									
3.5	4997674									
4.0	4999683									
4.5	4999966									
5.0	4999997133									

* This table was adapted, by permission, from F. C. Kent, "Elements of Statistics," McGraw-Hill Book Company, Inc., New York, 1924.

A more complete table is "Tables of Normal Probability Functions," National Bureau of Standards, Washington, 1953.

Table III. Maximum Deviations for Chauvenet's Criterion

For each value of N (N = number of observations) the table gives the value of d_i/σ such that the probability of occurrence of deviations *larger than* the given value is $1/2N$.

N	d_i/σ	N	d_i/σ
5	1.65	30	2.39
6	1.73	40	2.49
7	1.81	50	2.57
8	1.86	60	2.64
9	1.91	80	2.74
10	1.96	100	2.81
12	2.04	150	2.93
14	2.10	200	3.02
16	2.15	300	3.14
18	2.20	400	3.23
20	2.24	500	3.29
25	2.33	1000	3.48

Table IV. Values of χ^{2}*

The table gives values of χ^{2} which have various probabilities of being *exceeded* by a sample taken from the given parent distribution. The number of degrees of freedom is ν. To illustrate: For a sample with 10 degrees of freedom, the probability is 0.99 that it will have $\chi^{2} \geq 2.558$ and 0.001 that $\chi^{2} \geq 29.588$.

ν	Probability										
	0.99	0.98	0.95	0.90	0.80	0.20	0.10	0.05	0.02	0.01	0.001
1	$0.0^{3}157$	$0.0^{3}628$	0.00393	0.0158	0.0642	1.642	2.706	3.841	5.412	6.635	10.827
2	0.0201	0.0404	0.103	0.211	0.446	3.219	4.605	5.991	7.824	9.210	13.815
3	0.115	0.185	0.352	0.584	1.005	4.642	6.251	7.815	9.837	11.341	16.268
4	0.297	0.429	0.711	1.064	1.649	5.989	7.779	9.488	11.668	13.277	18.465
5	0.554	0.752	1.145	1.610	2.343	7.289	9.236	11.070	13.388	15.086	20.517
6	0.872	1.134	1.635	2.204	3.070	8.558	10.645	12.592	15.033	16.812	22.457
7	1.239	1.564	2.167	2.833	3.822	9.803	12.017	14.067	16.622	18.475	24.322
8	1.646	2.032	2.733	3.490	4.594	11.030	13.362	15.507	18.168	20.090	26.125
9	2.088	2.532	3.325	4.168	5.380	12.242	14.684	16.919	19.679	21.666	27.877
10	2.558	3.059	3.940	4.865	6.179	13.442	15.987	18.307	21.161	23.209	29.588
11	3.053	3.609	4.575	5.578	6.989	14.631	17.275	19.675	22.618	24.725	31.264
12	3.571	4.178	5.226	6.304	7.807	15.812	18.549	21.026	24.054	26.217	32.909
13	4.107	4.765	5.892	7.042	8.634	16.985	19.812	22.362	25.472	27.688	34.528
14	4.660	5.368	6.571	7.790	9.467	18.151	21.064	23.685	26.873	29.141	36.123
15	5.229	5.985	7.261	8.547	10.307	19.311	22.307	24.996	28.259	30.578	37.697
16	5.812	6.614	7.962	9.312	11.152	20.465	23.542	26.296	29.633	32.000	39.252
17	6.408	7.255	8.672	10.085	12.002	21.615	24.769	27.587	30.995	33.409	40.790
18	7.015	7.906	9.390	10.865	12.857	22.760	25.989	28.869	32.346	34.805	42.312
19	7.633	8.567	10.117	11.651	13.716	23.900	27.204	30.144	33.687	36.191	43.820
20	8.260	9.237	10.851	12.443	14.578	25.038	28.412	31.410	35.020	37.566	45.315
21	8.897	9.915	11.591	13.240	15.445	26.171	29.615	32.671	36.343	38.932	46.797
22	9.542	10.600	12.338	14.041	16.314	27.301	30.813	33.924	37.659	40.289	48.268
23	10.196	11.293	13.091	14.848	17.187	28.429	32.007	35.172	38.968	41.638	49.728
24	10.856	11.992	13.848	15.659	18.062	29.553	33.196	36.415	40.270	42.980	51.179
25	11.524	12.697	14.611	16.473	18.940	30.675	34.382	37.652	41.566	44.314	52.620
26	12.198	13.409	15.379	17.292	19.820	31.795	35.563	38.885	42.856	45.642	54.052
27	12.879	14.125	16.151	18.114	20.703	32.912	36.741	40.113	44.140	46.963	55.476
28	13.565	14.847	16.928	18.939	21.588	34.027	37.916	41.337	45.419	48.278	56.893
29	14.256	15.574	17.708	19.768	22.475	35.139	39.087	42.557	46.693	49.588	58.302
30	14.953	16.306	18.493	20.599	23.364	36.250	40.256	43.773	47.962	50.892	59.703

* This table is reproduced in abridged form from Table IV of Fisher and Yates, "Statistical Tables for Biological, Agricultural, and Medical Research," published by Oliver & Boyd, Ltd., Edinburgh, by permission of the authors and publishers.

Table V. Correlation Coefficients*

The table gives values of the correlation coefficient r which have certain probabilities of being *exceeded* for observations of variables whose parent distributions are independent. The number of pairs of observations is N. To illustrate: for a sample of 10 pairs of observations on unrelated variables, the probability is 0.10 that it will have $r \geq 0.549$, and the probability is 0.001 that $r \geq 0.875$.

N	Probability				
	0.10	0.05	0.02	0.01	0.001
3	0.988	0.997	0.999	1.000	1.000
4	0.900	0.950	0.980	0.990	0.999
5	0.805	0.878	0.934	0.959	0.992
6	0.729	0.811	0.882	0.917	0.974
7	0.669	0.754	0.833	0.874	0.951
8	0.621	0.707	0.789	0.834	0.925
10	0.549	0.632	0.716	0.765	0.872
12	0.497	0.576	0.658	0.708	0.823
15	0.441	0.514	0.592	0.641	0.760
20	0.378	0.444	0.516	0.561	0.679
30	0.307	0.362	0.423	0.464	0.572
40	0.264	0.312	0.367	0.403	0.502
60	0.219	0.259	0.306	0.337	0.422
80	0.188	0.223	0.263	0.291	0.366
100	0.168	0.199	0.235	0.259	0.327

* This table is adapted from Table VI of Fisher and Yates, "Statistical Tables for Biological, Agricultural, and Medical Research," published by Oliver & Boyd, Ltd., Edinburgh, by permission of the authors and publishers.

BIBLIOGRAPHY

Following are a few references for readers who want to pursue further some of the topics of this book. This is not intended to be an exhaustive list of the literature, but a suggestion of a few places to look for more information. Some of the books suppose considerably more mathematical sophistication on the part of the reader than the present volume.

Dixon, W. J., and F. J. Massey, Jr.: "Introduction to Statistical Analysis," 2d ed., McGraw-Hill Book Company, Inc., New York, 1957.

Fry, Thornton C.: "Probability and Its Engineering Uses," D. Van Nostrand Company, Inc., Princeton, N.J., 1928.

Hoel, Paul G.: "Introduction to Mathematical Statistics," 2d ed., John Wiley & Sons, Inc., New York, 1954.

Jeffreys, Harold: "Theory of Probability," Oxford University Press, New York, 1948.

Lindsay, Robert B., and Henry Margenau: "Foundations of Physics," John Wiley & Sons, Inc., New York, 1936 (reprinted by Dover Publications, Inc., New York).

Munroe, Marshall E.: "The Theory of Probability," McGraw-Hill Book Company, Inc., New York, 1951.

Parratt, Lyman G.: "Probability and Experimental Errors in Science," John Wiley & Sons, Inc., New York, 1961.

Pearson, Karl: "Tables for Statisticians and Biometricians," 3d ed., Cambridge University Press, New York, 1930.

Worthing, Archie, and Joseph Geffner: "Treatment of Experimental Data," John Wiley & Sons, Inc., New York, 1943.

ANSWERS TO PROBLEMS

CHAPTER I

1. (a) -8.02%
   (b) -0.366%
2. (a) 0.0402%
   (b) 8.5×10^{-8}
3. Increases
4. 40 mph; no, 20 mph
5. 4%
6. 20.13 lb
7. (a) 0.5×10^{-8}
   (b) 0.005
9. $\frac{1}{2}n(n-1)(\delta/A)^2$
10. (a) 1.003
    (b) 1.002
    (c) 1.002
11. (a) 0.2 cm, 0.2 cm
    (b) 0.0019; 0.040
12. (a) $\theta = 0$
    (b) $\theta = 45°$

13. (a) 0.30 m/sec^2;
        0.10 m/sec^2
    (b) T
14. $\Delta F_x = -F \sin \theta \, \Delta\theta$
    $\Delta F_y = F \cos \theta \, \Delta\theta$
    $\Delta F_x/F_x = -\tan \theta \, \Delta\theta$
    $\Delta F_y/F_y = \cot \theta \, \Delta\theta$
15. (a) 0.005
    (b) 2×10^{-4}
    (c) 10^{-4}
    (d) 0.1
    (e) 0.04
16. $m = 3,\ \sigma = \sqrt{2},\ \alpha = \frac{6}{5}$
17. (a) 3.50
    (b) 4.17
    (c) 3.50
18. $\sigma = 0.0024,\ \alpha = 0.0018$
20. Standard deviation
21. $\alpha = e/2,\ \sigma = e/\sqrt{3}$

CHAPTER II

1. $\frac{8}{76}$; yes, $\frac{1}{8}$
2. (a) $\frac{5}{6}$
   (b) $(\frac{5}{6})^2$
   (c) $(\frac{5}{6})^3$
   (d) 0
3. 2, 3, 4, 5, 6;
   $\frac{1}{4}, \frac{1}{3}, \frac{5}{18}, \frac{1}{9}, \frac{1}{36}$
4. $\frac{1}{64}, \frac{3}{64}, \frac{3}{32}, \frac{5}{32}, \frac{3}{16},$
   $\frac{3}{16}, \frac{5}{32}, \frac{3}{32}, \frac{3}{64}, \frac{1}{64}$
5. 0.706
6. $\frac{1}{1326}$

7. $\frac{9}{29}, \frac{153}{203}, 1$
8. $\frac{1}{2}, \frac{1}{3}, \frac{1}{6}$; yes
9. $\frac{9}{50}$
10. (a) 0.28
    (b) 0.010
    (c) 0.060
11. 0.349, 0.388, 0.263
12. Roughly 20%
13. $\frac{1}{6}, \frac{5}{36}, \frac{25}{216}, (\frac{1}{6})(\frac{5}{6})^n$
14. 252

15. 27,405
16. 945
17. 231,525
18. $\frac{1}{270}$, 725

19. 52!/39!13!;
    no, $4 \times$ 52!/39!13!
20. $\frac{1}{4165}$; no
22. 0.614

CHAPTER III

1. $\frac{1}{64}$, $\frac{3}{32}$, $\frac{15}{64}$, $\frac{5}{16}$, $\frac{15}{64}$, $\frac{3}{32}$, $\frac{1}{64}$; yes
2. $\frac{1}{6}$; $\frac{625}{1296}$, $\frac{500}{1296}$, $\frac{150}{1296}$, $\frac{20}{1296}$, $\frac{1}{1296}$, 0
3. 0.887, 0.107, 0.006
4. $4\,N$, $2\,N$, 0, $2\,S$, $4\,S$; $\frac{1}{16}$, $\frac{1}{4}$, $\frac{3}{8}$, $\frac{1}{4}$, $\frac{1}{16}$
5. For m blocks north, $P_m = N!/(N/2 + m/2)!(N/2 - m/2)!2^N$
6. 0; $N^{1/2}$
7. $4\,N$, $2\,N$, 0, $2\,S$, $4\,S$; $\frac{1}{256}$, $\frac{12}{256}$, $\frac{54}{256}$, $\frac{108}{256}$, $\frac{81}{256}$
8. For m blocks north,

$$P_m = \frac{N!}{\left(\dfrac{N+m}{2}\right)! \left(\dfrac{N-m}{2}\right)!} \left(\frac{1}{4}\right)^{(m+N)/2} \left(\frac{3}{4}\right)^{(N-m)/2}$$

9. $N/2$ blocks south; $(3N/4)^{1/2}$
10. (b) $\bar{n} = 73$; $\sigma = 27$
    (c) 61
11. 7.8, 2.0
12. 0.135, 0.270, 0.270, 0.180, 0.090, 0.036, 0.012, 0.003, 0.001; 8
13. 1.78, 1.36; 1.33
16. 0.632
17. 1.3×10^{-9}; very unlikely
18. 0.0014; coin is probably asymmetric

19. $\alpha = (2/\pi)^{1/2}\, \sigma$
20. 0.383
21. 0.674 σ; no; 0
22. 3, 1.22
23. (a) 0.175
    (b) 0.338
24. (b) b/π
    (c) m
    (d) Infinite
25. (b) $2b/\pi$
    (c) m
    (d) $b(4/\pi - 1)^{1/2}$
26. 0, $A/\sqrt{2}$, $4\,Af$, $\sqrt{2}\,\pi Af$

CHAPTER IV

1. 7.6×10^{-4}
2. 0.0114
3. $3N$

4. $\bar{x} = (\bar{x})_1/4 + 3(\bar{x})_2/4$
   $1/\sigma_m^2 = N/\sigma_1^2 + 3N/\sigma_2^2$
7. 0.22 m/sec²

Answers to Problems

8. (a) 0.023 in., 0.017 in.
   (b) $l = 11.000 \pm 0.012$ in.,
       $w = 8.500 \pm 0.006$ in.
   (c) $A = 93.50 \pm 0.11$ in.^{2}

9. No; difference is much larger than σ

10. 0.83%; e

11. (a) 0.900 ± 0.095
    (b) $64 \pm 12°$

13. $(a/N)^{1/2}$

14. $R = \Sigma V_i^2 / \Sigma V_i I_i$

15. $x = 0.96$, $y = 0.015$

16. $\alpha = 30\tfrac{2}{3}°$
    $\beta = 61\tfrac{2}{3}°$
    $\gamma = 87\tfrac{2}{3}°$
    if all errors have same
    normal distribution

17.
$$s_0 = \frac{\begin{vmatrix} \Sigma s & \Sigma t & \Sigma t^2 \\ \Sigma st & \Sigma t^2 & \Sigma t^3 \\ \Sigma st^2 & \Sigma t^3 & \Sigma t^4 \end{vmatrix}}{\Delta}$$

$$v_0 = \frac{\begin{vmatrix} N & \Sigma s & \Sigma t^2 \\ \Sigma t & \Sigma st & \Sigma t^3 \\ \Sigma t^2 & \Sigma st^2 & \Sigma t^4 \end{vmatrix}}{\Delta}$$

$$g = \frac{\begin{vmatrix} N & \Sigma t & \Sigma s \\ \Sigma t & \Sigma t^2 & \Sigma st \\ \Sigma t^2 & \Sigma t^3 & \Sigma st^2 \end{vmatrix}}{\Delta}$$

where $\Delta = \begin{vmatrix} N & \Sigma t & \Sigma t^2 \\ \Sigma t & \Sigma t^2 & \Sigma t^3 \\ \Sigma t^2 & \Sigma t^3 & \Sigma t^4 \end{vmatrix}$

18. $y = 1.34x - 0.29$,
    if y errors are normal and
    x errors negligible

19. $\dfrac{N\Sigma I_i C_i - (\Sigma I_i)(\Sigma C_i)}{N\Sigma I_i^2 - (\Sigma I_i)^2}$

20. $3\Sigma i C_i / N(N+1)(2N+1)$

INDEX

Mistakes, 3, 77

Most probable value, 104–105, 108–110
  standard deviation of, 92–95, 105–109
  for straight line constants, 120–121

Normal distribution (*see* Gauss distribution)
Normal equations, 118–120, 124–126
Normal error function (*see* Gauss distribution)
Normalization, binomial distribution, 54
  Gauss distribution, 69–70, 158–159
  Poisson distribution, 60
  probability distribution, 40, 60–61, 68–69

Observation equations, 116–117, 124–126
  nonlinear, 125

Parameters of distributions, 59–60, 66–73
Parent distribution, 45
  comparison with sample distribution, 80–82
Partial derivative, 6–7
Per cent standard deviation, 17–18

Permutations, 29–30
Poisson distribution, 57–64
  examples of, 57–58, 61–64
  mean of, 60–61
  normalization of, 60
  relation to binomial distribution, 58–59
  standard deviation of, 61
  variance of, 61
Precision, 3
  of the mean, 95–96
Principle, of least squares, 102, 117
  (*See also* Method of least squares)
  of maximum likelihood, 103–104, 107–112, 117
Probability, balls in an urn, 27–28
  compound, 25–27
  definition of, 23–25
  for dice, 25–27
  flipping pennies, 23–25
  meaning of, 23–28
Probability distribution, for continuous variable, 66–71
  examples of, 39–44
  mean of, 42–43
  meaning of, 39–42
  normalization of, 40, 60–61, 68–69
  standard deviation of, 44
  variance of, 44
  (*See also* Binomial distribution; Gauss distribution; Poisson distribution)

McGRAW-HILL PAPERBACKS

E. Bright Wilson, Jr.: AN INTRODUCTION
TO SCIENTIFIC RESEARCH

Henry Margenau: THE NATURE OF
PHYSICAL REALITY

D. N. deG. Allen: RELAXATION METHODS
IN ENGINEERING AND SCIENCE

Paul E. Machovina: A MANUAL FOR THE
SLIDE RULE

Lyman M. Kells, Willis F. Kern, James R. Bland:
LOG AND TRIG TABLES

Farrington Daniels: MATHEMATICAL
PREPARATION FOR PHYSICAL CHEMISTRY

Hardy Cross and Robert C. Goodpasture:
ENGINEERS AND IVORY TOWERS

W. Frederick Cottrell: ENERGY AND SOCIETY

H. V. Anderson: CHEMICAL CALCULATIONS

J. V. Uspensky: INTRODUCTION TO
MATHEMATICAL PROBABILITY

George R. Stibitz and Jules A. Larrivee:
MATHEMATICS AND COMPUTERS

Martin Gardner: LOGIC MACHINES AND
DIAGRAMS

Eric T. Bell: MATHEMATICS: QUEEN AND
SERVANT OF SCIENCE

McGRAW-HILL PAPERBACKS

Donald H. Menzel, Howard Mumford Jones, and
Lyle G. Boyd: WRITING A TECHNICAL
PAPER

Clifford T. Morgan and James Deese: HOW
TO STUDY

Arthur Beiser: THE WORLD OF PHYSICS